Tishrei

Shabbat Shuva
essays in preparation
for Yom Kippur

Thoughts

RABBI BEN TZION GREENBERGER

Cover design by: Rivkah Lewis

Book Production Services by:
Torah Typing
19/4 Yitzchak Ben Dor Street
Jerusalem 93281 Israel
info@torahtyping.com
www.torahtyping.com

Distributed by:
Ezekiel Publishing
(a division of Torah Typing)

Printed in Israel

Tishrei

Shabbat Shuva
essays in preparation
for Yom Kippur

Thoughts

RABBI BEN TZION GREENBERGER

Table of Contents

Introduction

ᔥᔨ

IT HAS BEEN A great privilege for me to serve as the Rav of Bet Knesset Mitzpe Nevo in Maale Adumim for approximately the past 20 years. I have delivered many hundreds of *shiurim* over these many years, *u-mi-kol melamdai hiskalti* – I have learned much and derived much satisfaction from the opportunity to share ideas of Torah with my listeners.

Approximately 12 years ago, at the "insistence" of Shelly Wolgel, one of our "veteran" members, I agreed to deliver a *Shabbat Teshuvah derasha* in English for the growing number of residents of Mitzpe Nevo, and of Maaleh Adumim in general, who wished to hear a *derasha* before Yom Kippur in their native tongue. With untiring perseverance, Shelly made it happen, and this *derasha* has become a permanent fixture in our *shul*.

This volume represents the fruits of these annual encounters, in which I have sought to enrich our understanding and experience of the *Aseret Yemei Teshuvah* and Yom Kippur. In this regard, I note with great humility and *yir'at ha-kavod* the significant influence of Ha-Rav Yosef Dov Soloveitchik *ztz"l* on my understanding and appreciation of the major themes of these holy days. Even a cursory perusal of these pages will reveal the presence of "The Rav" in much of what I have had to say over the years.

I should stress that this volume is not an academic treatise, nor even a structured *chibbur torani*, but rather a transcription of the *derashot* themselves as delivered in our *shul*. The number of footnotes and references has been kept to a minimum in order to allow the reader to "flow" with the ideas reflected in the *derashot* without distraction.

I wish to dedicate this volume to the three generations who have shaped my life and inspired my path. My parents, Herman and Golde Greenberger *z"l*, set me upon the path I have striven to travel my entire life. I am indebted to my dear wife, Chaya, without whose singular inspiration and support I would never have succeeded in my quest. Finally, my beloved children - Moshe, Tzippy, Sara, Chaim, and Avital – as well as their spouses, have brought me such joy and *nachas*, leaving me assured that our family's foundations, its values and its aspirations, will indeed carry on.

Yehi Ratzon she-tishreh Shechinotcha be-ma'aseh yadenu.

Ben Tzion Greenberger
Maaleh Adumim, Israel
Elul 5772

Those Who Dwell
in Your House

ALTHOUGH THERE ARE SLIGHT variations in the *Selichot* that we recite every day starting from before Rosh Hashana, every recitation begins with *Ashrei*. There is a simple halachic explanation for this – we say a *perek* of *Tehillim* so that we can say *Kaddish* before *Selichot*. But why *Ashrei*? What is the significance of this particular *perek* during the *Aseret Yemei Teshuva* and, for that matter, throughout the year?

Another interesting phenomenon one may notice in the *Selichot* recited up until Yom Kippur is the refrain which we recite after the individual *piyutim*. Following the first *piyut*, the refrain is "*Kel erech apayim ve-rav chesed ve-emet*," which is the same refrain that we recite in the daily *Tachanun*. Following the second *piyut* and thereafter, the refrain changes to "*Kel Melech yoshev al kisei rachamim*." On Yom Kippur,

in contrast, we begin immediately with "*Kel Melech yoshev*."
What is the significance of this?

❧ *ASHREI YOSHVEI BEITECHA – ASHREI HA-AM SHE-KACHA LO*

The *perek* of *Tehillim* that we refer to as "*Ashrei*" is really
not one single *perek*. The first *pasuk* – "*Ashrei yoshvei beitecha*"
– is from *perek* 84; the second *pasuk* – "*Ashrei ha-am she-
kacha lo*" – is from *perek* 144. The majority of the *pesukim*,
beginning with "*Tehillah le-David*," are found in *perek* 145,
while the final *pasuk* – "*Va-anachnu nivarech Kah*" – is found
in *Hallel*. Why did *Chazal* choose to form this *tefillah*, which
we recite three times a day in our daily *tefillot* and countless
more times throughout the year, out of a patchwork of
different *perakim*?

The mishnah in *Berachot* (30b) teaches:

> *Ein omdin le-hitpallel ela mitoch kovod rosh* – one
> may only begin to pray in a serious mood. The early
> *Chassidim* used to wait an hour before they prayed
> so that they would have proper *kavana* towards
> their father in heaven.

These "*chassidim ha-rishonim*" would come to *shul* early
in order to prepare themselves for *tefillah* and attain the
proper mindset of *koved rosh*. In this manner, they did not
rush into *davening*, but rather had time to contemplate what
they were about to do. The *gemara* (32b) explains that the
source for this practice is the verse "*Ashrei yoshvei beitecha*,"
"Praised are those who sit in Your house." Rashi clarifies that
only after you are "*yoshvei beitecha*" is the second part of the

verse possible – "*od yehallucha sela.*" Only after first sitting in *shul* can you properly praise *Hashem*.[1]

Rabbi Yehoshua ben Levi adds that it is also necessary to wait an hour after the *tefillah*, as the *pasuk* says, "*Ach tzaddikim yodu li-shmecha, yeishvu yesharim mi-panecha,*" "The righteous will praise Your name, and the straight ones will sit before You;" after praising *Hashem*, we must once again "sit" before Him. It is not appropriate to run out of *shul* immediately after *davening*.

The *gemara* notes that the *chassidim ha-rishonim* apparently spent nine hours a day on *tefillah*, given that they waited an hour before and after each prayer three times a day! When did they have time to learn Torah? When were they supposed to get any work done? The *gemara* concludes that because they were *chassidim*, righteous observers of the *mitzvot*, their Torah was preserved and their work was taken care of.

We find an additional *halacha* connected to this idea of waiting an hour before and after *tefillah*, brought in the name of R. Chisda (*Berachot* 8a), that one should go through two doors when he enters a *shul*. Rashi explains that this means that before beginning one's prayers, one must enter the *shul* at least the distance it takes to cover the width of two doors. It is not appropriate to *daven* right next to the door of the *shul*, as if he is preparing to exit at the first possible opportunity. Such behavior indicates a lack of respect and demonstrates that one does not really want to be there at all; he is simply absolving

---

1 The *gemara* similarly learns from this *pasuk* that if one enters a *shul* for a reason other than *tefillah* – to speak to someone or retrieve an item, for example – he must at least sit down in the *shul* to demonstrate respect for the *kedushat beit ha-knesset*.

himself of his responsibility in as rapid a manner as possible.

Shulchan Aruch (*Orach Hayyim 90:20*) cites Rashi's explanation, ruling that one should enter into a *shul* a distance of at least eight *tefachim* before *davening,* so that it does not appear as though he wishes to rush out. If, however, the only seat left in *shul* is next to the door, there is no problem with sitting there, as this does not reflect any disrespect. Others explain that if one sits near the door, he is liable to become distracted by what he sees through the window, and for this reason he should move further away from the door. In that case, if the door faces an area where there are no distractions, there would not be a problem sitting there. Finally, *Shulchan Aruch* cites a view that the *gemara* means that one should prepare himself for prayer the length of *time* it takes to walk through two doors. This fits in well with the approach of the *chassidim ha-rishonim*, who used to wait an hour before beginning to pray.

Mishna Berura explains that while the *chassidim ha-rishonim* were capable of waiting an hour before praying, most people simply don't have the time. It is for this reason that the *gemara* offers an alternate option of the time it takes to walk through two doors, which is the equivalent of a few minutes. This is a tangible expression of preparation before and after *tefillah.*

Obviously, if someone generally runs into *shul* with enough time to catch *Hodu,* that isn't exactly what the *chassidim ha-rishonim* – or the *Shulchan Aruch* – had in mind. And if someone runs out sometime before the *Shir Shel Yom,* that's clearly also not optimal, even if it is unfortunately sometimes necessary.

Rav Soloveitchik explained that the idea expressed in the commitment of the *chassidim ha-rishonim* is a concept reflected in many other areas of *Halacha* as well. *Kedusha* demands *hachana*, preparation. One cannot simply leap from *chol* to *kodesh*; a transition is necessary between profane and sacred. Thus, we always add "*mei-chol al ha-kodesh*" before and after Shabbat, as well as on Yom Kippur. The entire notion of *Sefirat Ha-Omer* is one of preparation – *hachana* for *Matan Torah* at the end of the count. When *shemitta* was *de-orayta*, the *beit din* also conducted a *sefirah* of the *shnot ha-shemitta* in preparation for the upcoming *kedusha*.

The Rav noted that the concept of *hachana* for *kedusha* is actually derived from the Torah. Moshe Rabbeinu instructed *Bnei Yisrael* that before *Matan Torah*, they must prepare themselves - "*hitkadshu*" - for three days. The Targum translates this as "*hazminu*," which means preparation in halachic terminology.

If one were to leap from his home directly into the *beit ha-knesset* without even a thought, he would be forgetting that *kedusha* requires *hachana*. This is the idea expressed in the *pasuk*, "*Ashrei yoshvei beitecha*."

If we look more closely at the *perek* from which this verse is taken, we can glean an even greater understanding of its significance. *Perek* 84 of *Tehillim* describes our longing for the "dwelling places of *Hashem*." "*Mah yedidot mishkenotecha Hashem Tzevakot*" – How beloved are Your *mishkenot*, the places where Your *kedusha* rests! "*Nichsefa ve-gam kaltah nafshi le-chatzrot Hashem*" – my soul yearns for the courtyards of *Hashem*! "*Gam tzipor matza bayit*" – even the bird, who is free to roam the skies, always finds its way back home. "*U-dror ken*

la, asher shatah efrocheha" – even the freest of birds has a nest
in which its chicks are found. Rav Soloveitchik noted that if
you move a bird's eggs to a different nest, it will no longer sit
on those eggs; in order for a bird to feel its maternal instincts,
it has to be in its place, its nest. We humans also have places
we call home; but nevertheless there is only one place that we
view as our true home: "*Et mizbechotecha Hashem Tzevakot
malki ve-Elokai*" – *Hashem*'s altars.

At that point, it is in the next *passuk* that we declare,
"*Ashrei yoshvei beitecha, od yehalleucha sela.*" We properly
praise *Hashem* when we are "*yoshev*" in His house – not just
sitting there, but dwelling there as residents.

According to the Rav, this *mizmor Tehillim* was recited
when the *olei regel* were preparing to leave Yerushalayim and
return home.[2] As they prepare to depart, they declare how
difficult it is for them to leave their true home. "*Nichsefa ve-
gam kalta nafshi le-chatzrot Hashem*" – I'm only just leaving,
but I already yearn from what I'm leaving behind.

Chazal, in their great wisdom, wished to articulate the
idea that entry into *kedusha* demands mental preparation,
and they therefore "planted" the *pasuk* of "*Ashrei yoshvei
beitecha*" at the beginning of *Pesukei De-Zimra*. In order to

---

2 There is similarly a particular *mizmor* that was recited when pilgrims arrived
in *Yerusalayim* – "*samachti be-omrim li beit Hashem neileich. Omdot hayu
ragleinu be-sha'arayich Yerushalayim*" (*perek* 122). It is generally assumed that
this was the *perek* recited by the *olei regel*, but it is also possible that it was
more commonly said by those bringing *bikkurim* to the *Beit Ha-Mikdash*.
For this reason, the *pasuk* writes, "*samachti be-omrim li*," "I rejoiced when
they told me" to go to Yerushalayim. The *Rosh Ma'amad* would declare when
it was the appropriate time to bring a particular fruit as *bikkurim*; thus, the
people were told when to go.

enter the proper mindset of *tefillah* – "*od yehallucha sela*" – we must first become conscious of the *kedusha* of the place in which we sit.[3]

It is interesting that *Chazal* chose to place this *pasuk* at the very beginning of *davening* instead of at the end. After all, the *perek* from which it was taken was recited upon leaving the *Beit Ha-Mikdash*, expressing how difficult it is to part. By placing it at the start of our *tefillot*, they remind us that we can fulfill our yearning for *kedusha* right now; we don't have to wait until after *shul* is over and we're in the middle of our daily drudgery to think about how great it was to really connect to *davening*. We don't have to wait until a situation of *nichsefa ve-gam kalta nafshi*, when we feel great loss and pain, to recognize what we have right now. *Chazal* are telling us that our yearning for *kedusha* exists now, if we take notice and feel it.

Now that we understand why the *pasuk* of "*Ashrei yoshvei beitecha*" was placed before *Tehilla Le-David*, we must contemplate the significance of the second "out-of-place" verse: "*Ashrei ha-am she-kacha lo, ashrei ha-am she-Hashem Elokav.*" This is the last *pasuk* in *perek* 144, immediately preceding *Tehilla Le-David* in *perek* 145. Why do we carry

---

3 Tosfot note that in the time of the *Ge'onim*, it was customary to recite seven different *pesukim* from *Tehillim* that begin with the word "*ashrei*" – such as "*Ashrei ha-ish asher lo halach be-atzat resha'im*" and "*Ashrei temimei derech*" – before reciting *Tehilla Le-David*. Apparently, the idea was to express how fortunate we view ourselves as we begin our praises of *Hashem*. By Tosfot's era, however, it was already established that only the *pasuk* of "*Ashrei yoshvei beitecha*" was recited. The focus is not the word "*ashrei*," but rather "*yoshvei beitecha*" – we identify ourselves completely with the *kedusha* of the *makom*, after which we can proceed to praise *Hashem*.

over a *pasuk* from the previous *perek*?

To answer this question, the Rav cited another *gemara* in *Brachot* (17a), which describes what the students would recite when they would leave the *beit midrash* of Rav Chisda to return home – "*Alufeinu mesubalim, ein peretz ve-ein yotzeit ve-ein tzevacha be-rechovoteinu*" (*Tehillim* 144:14). The *Amora'im* explain that this means that our *alufim*, the masters of Torah, are *mesubalim be-yissurim*, suffer greatly. The Rav explained that just as there is a special *perek* of *Tehillim* recited upon leaving the *Beit Ha-Mikdash*, there is a special *perek* recited by *talmidim* upon leaving the *beit midrash*, in which they express their suffering upon leaving a *makom Torah*. Essentially, *perek* 144 expresses the same idea as *perek* 84 – that we feel pain and yearning upon leaving a place of holiness. *Chazal* therefore joined the last *pasuk* of this *perek* to the *pasuk* from *perek* 84 as introductions to *Tehilla Le-David*, so that we identify the *shul* we are in as a *makom tefillah* and a *makom Torah*.[4]

The above therefore explains why *Chazal* decided that "*Ashrei yoshvei beitecha*" should be the opening line of every recitation of *Selichot*, because no other *tefillah* is better suited to express our yearning for *kedusha*.

We praise the person who is "*yoshev*" in *Hashem's* holy places, who dwells there and who views it as his permanent home – not someone who simply happens to "sit" there. We

---

4 Clearly, there was also a poetic decision at work, as both verses begin with the word "*Ashrei*." Similarly, the *pasuk* appended to the end of *Tehilla Le-David* – "*Ve-anachnu nivarech Kah mei-atah ve-ad olam hallelukah*" – was chosen for stylistic reasons, as *Chazal* wanted the end of *Ashrei* to begin the series of "*Hallelukah*"s.

would like *Hashem* to similarly be "*yoshev*" on His Throne of Mercy, to view that as His proper place. But during the *yemei Selichot*, He does not necessarily choose to do so; He only sits on the *kisei rachamim* if we arouse His compassion. We therefore begin by describing *Hashem* as "*Kel erech apayim.*" It is only after we recite the 13 Attributes of Mercy that He becomes "*Kel melech yoshev al kisei rachamim.*" On Yom Kippur, however, *Hashem*'s permanent place is the *kisei rachamim* from the very beginning of that holy day. The day itself – the *itzumo shel yom* – creates the status of mercy that brings repentance. Even before we recite the 13 Attributes, *Hashem* is already sitting upon his Throne of Mercy, waiting for us; all that we need do is rise to meet Him.

❧ THE *ASERET YEMEI TESHUVA* AND YEARNING FOR *KEDUSHA*

On a practical level, the message of *Ashrei* is that we should focus a bit more consciously on our *davening* in *shul*. We are often frustrated that our day-to-day lives interfere with the kind of connection to *kedusha* that we would optimally like to experience. On days when we don't work, the *davening* experience is often very different than on days that we do. When you "catch" the "early-bird" *minyan*, you are most likely not going to be imitating the *chassidim harishonim* very much! Unfortunately, we often find ourselves in situations in which we have to "catch" a *davening*, because our schedule and responsibilities – our jobs, our spouses, our children – simply do not allow us to do more. But at the very least, when we say "*Ashrei yoshvei beitecha*," we should feel the *ga'aguim* that *Am Yisrael* felt when they left the *Beit HaMikdash* or *beit midrash*. We should at least feel that something is missing, even if it is unavoidable.

If that is not possible during the year, we should at least try to focus on this point during the *Aseret Yemei Teshuva*. *Shulchan Aruch* writes that during this time, we should be *mehadder* in *mitzvot* even in areas that we know we will not be able to maintain during the entire year. Many people wonder why this is not blatant hypocrisy. Are we trying to "fool" *Ha-Kadosh Baruch Hu*? What is the point of being *machmir* during the *Aseret Yemei Teshuva* if you're going to return to your old ways after Simchat Torah?

This is, in fact, the classic *kitrug* of the *Satan*. The *gemara (Rosh Hashana 16b)* explains that we blow the *Tekiyot De-Miyushav*, the 30 blasts of the shofar before *Musaf* on Rosh Hashana, in order to confuse the *Satan*.[5] *Satan* comes before *Hashem* and argues that *Am Yisrael* only does the right thing in order to be *yotzei* their obligation. If *Hashem* commands us, we perform; if we are not commanded, we go about our business. We thus blow extra *tekkiot before* we are obligated to do so, in order to "confuse" the *Satan*'s argument and prove that we love the *mitzvot* and do not act only out of obligation. This is similarly the reason for our practice of beginning *Sefer Bereishit* on Simchat Torah immediately upon concluding *Ve-Zot Ha-Brahca*, even though the new *kriah* does not count towards the *aliyyot* of the day or the reading of *parshat Bereishit* itself, which will be done only

---

5 The only blasts required *min ha-din* are those blown during *Shmoneh Esrei* alongside *Malchiyot*, *Zichronot*, and *Shofarot*.

the following *shabbat*. The *Satan* claims that all we are interested in doing is finishing up our obligation – and then, it's off to the *kiddush*! Tomorrow, we will all revert to our daily routines, as if we had not just completed the Torah. We therefore immediately begin *Bereishit*, in order to prove the *Satan* wrong, and to prove to *Hashem* that we love the Torah and will start it again even though we are not obligated to do so at that moment.

How do we respond to *Satan's* argument regarding our practices during the *Aseret Yemei Teshuva*? After all, he would seem to be right; we don't intend to keep up the *chumrot* we take upon ourselves during this time! One possibility is that we are not really concerned about *Satan's* argument, because we believe that there is a certain benefit to these *hiddurim*. Maybe we'll get accustomed to them, and some will remain with us even after Yom Kippur; but even if they don't, these *hiddurim* demonstrate that *"nichsefa ve-gam kalta nafshi"* – we yearn to experience *kedusha* whenever we can. If we can experience a bit more during the *Aseret Yemei Teshuva*, there's nothing to be ashamed of. Every day that we add a little bit to our *kedusha* experience has value, in and of itself, even if we know that we will not be able to maintain that level throughout the year. In that sense, all of *Aseret Yemei Teshuva* is a *hachana* for entering the *kedusha* of Yom Kippur.[6]

---

6 Another *hachana* for Yom Kippur is the *Tefillah Zakah* recited just before *Kol Nidrei*, which is essentially a long *viduy*. The Rav was very *makpid* to recite this *tefillah* to fulfill the Ramban's view that *viduy* should be recited after the *seudah ha-mafseket*. It also serves as an appropriate *hachana* for the essential work we do during the entire day of Yom Yippur – recounting our sins in order to facilitate *teshuva*.

❧ THE JOY OF SUKKOT

Sfat Emet writes that on Sukkot, *Hashem* gives *Bnei Yisrael* a greater level of *simcha*. *"ve-Samachta be-chagecha"* is not merely a commandment to be happy and joyous during the chag; it is *Hashem's* promise to us to grant us happiness! He gives us this joy so that we can greet Him properly, as the *pasuk* says, *"Ashrei yoshvei beitecha."* Those who dwell in *Hashem's* house – His *sukka* – rejoice. *Hashem* promises that if we sit in the *sukka* and praise Him through the *lulav* and *Hallel*, we will be merit the special joy of the chag.

Sfat Emet notes that after the *Yamim Nora'im*, it is actually quite difficult to find joy without *Hashem's* help. In the *tefillot* of Rosh HaShana and Yom Kippur, we openly recognized that *Hashem* controls our destiny - *mi yichyeh u-mi yamut, mi ba-ra'ash u-mi ba-magefa* – and we cannot know where or when the next disaster may strike. We may emerge from our *davening* with a sense of *bitachon* that *Hashem* heard our pleas, but we are also well aware that He never promised that He would fulfill them as we would wish. *Hashem* is the *Shomei'a Tefillah*, not necessarily the *Ma'azin Tefillah*. We can only hope that He has heard us, but cannot assume that He will necessarily listen. We thus leave Yom Kippur with a certain sense of trepidation; we have no idea what *Hashem* will decree. Thus, *Sfat Emet* writes, if *Hashem* were not to grant us *simcha* on Sukkot, it would be difficult to be truly happy.

Accordingly, *Ashrei* not only expresses our *ga'agu'im* for *kedusha*, but it also serves as an "IOU" that we present to *Hashem* that He will deliver us the *simcha* of Sukkot. The blessing of *simcha* that we enjoy when we sit in our *sukkot*, the "houses" of *Hashem*, will then carry us throughout the days that follow.

Transitions in the Yom Kippur Machzor

ALTHOUGH YOM KIPPUR IS unique in incorporating five prayer services, *Chazal* actually viewed these *tefillot* as one unit of prayer. These are not discrete, independent periods of prayer, but rather components of one united day of prayer. It is perhaps for this reason that some *shuls* and *yeshivas* frown upon the idea of a break between *Musaf* and *Mincha*. All the *tefillot* are essentially one, and the various parts of that unit should not be disconnected from one another.

Rav Soloveitchik noted that this idea is accentuated in the first *piyut* that we recite on the night of Yom Kippur, "*Ya'aleh tachanunenu mei-erev, ve-yavo sha'avateinu mi-boker, ve-yeira'eh rinunenu ad arev.*" As we stand at the very beginning of the holiest day of the year, we are already thinking of its end, connecting *Ma'ariv* to *Ne'ilah*. Our prayers rise to

Hashem beginning "*mei-erev*," from nightfall, they continue to come before Him "*mi-boker*," from the morning, and they are seen before Him "*ad arev*," until Yom Kippur draws to a close. We are now beginning a process that will only end in twenty-four hours, at the *eit ne'ilat sha'ar*.[7] All of the *tefillot* are part of one process that leads up to the pinnacle of *Ne'ilah*, which constitutes a recapitulation of what we have said thus far and a plea that *Hashem* accept all of our *tefillot*. In fact, the Rav insists that since *Ne'ilah* is not an independent *tefillah*, if someone missed one of the other *tefillot* of the day, he may not recite *Ne'ilah*!

Despite this intrinsic unity in the *tefillot* of Yom Kippur, however, there are a number of transitions in the *machzor* that create dramatic contrasts. By studying these contrasts, we can achieve a greater sense of the messages that *Chazal* wished to impart to us.

❧ ADAM YESODO MEI-AFAR – EIN KITZVA LI-SHNOTECHA

Anyone who has sung *Ein Kitzva* to the feisty tune of a Napoleonic march is certainly acquainted with one of these stark contrasts. After intoning the somber reflections of *U-Netaneh Tokef* – "*mi yichyeh u-mi yamut*" – we conclude that man is finite; he is here today and gone tomorrow.

---

7 The Rav further notes that the verbs used in this *piyut* – "*ya'aleh*," "*ve-yavo*," and "*ve-yeira'eh*" – were chosen by the *paytan* to remind us of three *pesukim* that indicate that *Hashem* listens to the *tefillot* of *Am Yisrael*. When the Jewish People was suffering in Egypt, the *pasuk* tell us, "**va-ta'al** *sha'avatam*;" *Hashem* attests, "*tza'akat Bnei Yisrael* **ba'ah** *eilay*;" and *Hashem* recognizes their suffering, "**va-yar** *Elokim*."

"*Adam yesodo mei-afar ve-sofo le-afar*" – man is formed from the dust of the earth and, in the end, he will return to it. He is compared to "*cheres ha-nishbar*," broken pottery, to a "*chalom ya'uf*," a fleeting dream. We focus on our smallness, our utter dependence on *Hashem*'s grace, and the necessity of repentance to assure another year of life. And then all of a sudden, we sing a lively tune to *Ein Kitzva*. Indeed, the transition is so stark that it almost seems inappropriate.

The truth is, however, that our joyous tune makes sense given the context. If man were alone in the universe, if only our finitude made up creation, we would have to stop with the reflection of "*chalom ya'uf*," with a feeling of hopelessness. But man is not alone – "*Ve-ata hu melech Kel chai ve-kayam*," "But You are the King, the living and enduring God." While it is true that "*Adam yesodo mei-afar*," we rest assured that "*Ein kitzva li-shnotecha*." This provides a ray of hope for us, changing our despair into faith in the future. Our cheerful *niggun* reflects that we have been redeemed from the depths of despondency.

The *machzor* constructs this reversal in atmosphere through one stark transition; it builds a certain mood, gets to its depths, and suddenly creates a dramatic reversal.

❧ THE *AVODA* OF YOM KIPPUR

A major part of the *Musaf* of Yom Kippur consists of a very detailed description of the *avoda* that took place in the *Beit Ha-Mikdash* on that day. Why are the historic details of the *avoda* stressed so much?

On a basic level, one might argue that we recite the

korbanot due to the concept of "*u-nishalma parim sefateinu*" – our lips complete the *avoda* that we can no longer actually perform.[8] If that were the only reason, however, it would be difficult to understand why the *chazzan* introduces the *avoda* with the short *tefillah* of *Ochila La-Kel*, in which he implores *Hashem* to assist him in articulating himself properly. This same *tefillah* is recited before *Malchiot, Zichronot*, and *Shofarot* on Rosh Hashana; before the congregation coronates God, the *chazzan* asks for assistance in properly representing the *tzibbur*. If the *avoda* of Yom Kippur is essentially no different than *Musaf* on Shabbos, why is *Ochila La-Kel* appropriate at this juncture?

The Rav explained that the *avoda* is actually much more than a verbal replacement for the *korbanot*. It is rather a celebration of *Torah She-Be'al Peh*. The sequence of events on Yom Kippur as they actually took place in the *Beit Ha-Mikdash* was not consistent with the literal instructions of *Torah She-Bichtav*, as they were informed as well by the interpretations of *chazal* as expressed in *Torah She-Be'al Peh*. After performing the *avoda* according to the dictates of *Torah She-Be'al Peh*, the *kohen gadol* would read to the people the *parshiot* describing the *avoda*. Upon completion of this reading, he would declare, "*Yoter mi-mah she-karati*

---

8 The *gemara* in *Megillah* (31b) records a conversation between *Hashem* and Avraham Avinu in which Avraham expresses concern that his descendants will ultimately sin and be deserving of punishment, thus forfeiting their rights to the land – "*Ba-mah eida ki irashenu?*" *Hashem* tells Avraham to offer Him *korbanot*, symbolizing that *Bnei Yisrael* will be spared in the merit of their sacrifices. Avraham then questions what their merit will be after the *Beit Ha-Mikdash* is destroyed, and *Hashem* promises him that at that point, the recitation of the *parshiot* of the *korbanot* will replace the actual sacrifices.

lifneichem katuv kan" (*Yoma* 68b). The Rav explains that the people would be confused; why did the *kohen gadol* act in a different manner than dictated by the very verses that he just read? The *kohen gadol* would respond that *Torah She-Be'al Peh* demands more than what is written in the Torah, and that is why he acted differently than the *pesukim,* taken literally, demand of him.

Beit Ha-Levi explains that Yom Kippur is actually the *Yom Tov* of the *Torah She-Be'al Peh,* as it was the day on which the *Torah She-Be'al Peh* was given to *Bnei Yisrael.* When Moshe was given the first set of *luchot,* all of the content of *Torah She-Be'al Peh* was written upon them. *Yalkut Shimoni* tells us that following the *cheit ha-egel,* the letters disappeared; instead of holding a living, breathing Torah, Moshe was now carrying the dead weight of a rock, and he simply dropped the *luchot,* which were now too heavy. When the second *luchot* were given on Yom Kippur, the *Torah She-Be'al Peh* was no longer written upon them, but was rather transmitted orally. Thus, Yom Kippur is the holiday of *Torah She-Be'al Peh.*

The *avoda* on Yom Kippur is thus more than a stand-in for the actual sacrificial service. It is a celebration of the *Torah She-Be'al Peh*, and that celebration demands explanation. The *chazzan* thus asks for the necessary eloquence to convey this content, these ideas, to the *tzibbur.*

❧ FROM EXPERIENCE TO MOURNING

One of the starkest contrasts in the Yom Kippur *davening* takes place in the recitation of the *avoda* itself. Although the *avoda* begins as a technical description of the sacrificial order in the *Beit Ha-Mikdash*, it becomes increasingly experiential as the description goes on, giving the sense that this was not simply something that happened long ago, but that we sense it even now. In the beginning, the *avoda* uses the past tense to describe the events, as in, for example, "*ve-kach haya omer.*" As we get a greater and greater sense of what took place – bowing along with the *kohanim* and the people in response to hearing *Hashem*'s name – we suddenly shift to present tense, as we quote the *tefillah* that the *Kohen Gadol* would recite upon leaving the *Kodesh Ha-Kodashim*. The *avoda* is no longer simply a commemoration; we now ask for these very same things for ourselves, our families, and *Klal Yisrael*. We are then transported to the courtyard of the *Beit Ha-Mikdash* as we describe the glorious appearance of the *Kohen Gadol* at that sublime point – "*Mareh Kohen.*" The *avoda* is no longer a history lesson, and we sing this *piyut* to an uplifting *niggun* celebrating the sight that we see before our very eyes. We are ourselves experiencing the Yom Kippur of the *Beit Ha-Mikdash*.

The Rav used to say that one couldn't possibly talk to his father or grandfather, Rav Chaim of Brisk, at this point in the *tefillah*. They were no longer in Brisk, but rather in Yerushalayim, watching as the *Kohen Gadol* exited the *Kodesh Ha-Kodashim*.

But at this point, there is a drastic switch in the *machzor*. From the pinnacle of the ecstasy of *Mareh Kohen*, we are now transported to the depths of despair – "*Ashrei ayin ra'atah kol eleh, halo le'mishma ozen da'ava nafshenu.*" We are reminded that everything we have described – everything we have experienced – is no more, as the *Beit Ha-Mikdash* has been destroyed. The *simcha* of Yom Kippur swiftly changes into the mourning of Tisha B'Av. We cannot see the *Kohen Gadol* today because of our sins. Indeed, while our fathers' sins caused the destruction, our sins perpetuate it; as the *Yerushalmi* (*Yoma* 5a) famously states, any generation that does not rebuild the *Beit Ha-Mikdash* is held responsible for its destruction.

Although we can experience the glory of the *avoda* of Yom Kippur, although we can be transported to the *Kodesh Ha-Kodashim*, we can be there only *be-chorbano*, not *be-binyano*. For this reason, the *chazzan* must begin the *avoda* with *Ochila La-Kel*. Without *Hashem*'s help to open our hearts and minds, it would be too difficult to continue.

Yom Kippur is both a day of *kappara* and a day of *evel*, a time for us to consider all that we have lost. For this reason, we recite the *piyut* of the *asara harugei malchut*, developing a new theme of the terror and tragedy of *churban*. By building the excitement surrounding the *avoda*, the *paytan* creates a powerful effect as we sharply transition to the reality of destruction.

❧ LE-HITPALLEL IM HA-AVARYANIM – SHE-HECHEYANU

Another interesting transition takes place at the very beginning of the Yom Kippur service. *Kol Nidrei* is perhaps the most famous prayer of the year, but it is an extremely enigmatic one. Why do we solemnly chant what is essentially a legal cancelling of vows? Furthermore, we already performed *hatarat nedarim* before Rosh Hashana. Why is it necessary again? Finally, although we know that making unnecessary *nedarim* is not a positive practice, we surely have more weighty transgressions that would more appropriately serve as a focus for the opening *tefillah* of Yom Kippur. In fact, we just listed them in the *viduy* of *erev* Yom Kippur! Why are we focusing on our vows as we begin the Day of Atonement?

The Rav explained that *Kol Nidrei* represents the fundamental truth that the past can be changed. *Beit Din* is granted the ability to be *matir nedarim*, to erase one's *neder* as if it had never been made. A person may come before the court and explain, "Had I known then what I know now – how difficult it would be to keep this oath – I would never have made it!" He can thus retroactively take back what he said. *Teshuva* can similarly retroactively change the past, erasing the sins committed throughout the year. *Kol Nidrei* is thus an apt introduction to Yom Kippur, bringing us into the mindset that this day can change the past.

We begin *Kol Nidrei* by granting permission to all the admitted sinners – those who have already recited the *viduy* of *erev* Yom Kippur and who do not deny their sinful state – to join in the *tefillot*. On this day, it is permissible and worthwhile "*le-hitpallel im ha-avaryanim*," to pray with the sinners.

Strangely, immediately following *Kol Nidrei*, we recite the *bracha* of *She-Hecheyanu*. Usually, this *bracha* is recited in *Kiddush*, which is obviously not said on Yom Kippur, but it seems most inappropriate at this point. We just finished declaring that we are *avaryanim*, that we must dedicate ourselves to *teshuva*, and instead of transitioning into a related theme – perhaps the 13 *middot ha-rachamim* or *Avinu*

Malkeinu – we recite a joyous blessing thanking *Hashem*! What is this *bracha* doing here?

The answer is actually quite simple. After reciting *Kol Nidrei* and recognizing that *Hashem* can and will erase our sins retroactively, after imploring, "*Slach na le-avon ha-am ha-zeh ke-godel chasdecha*" and declaring the famous words, "*Va-Yomer Hashem salachti ke-devarecha*," the goal of Yom Kippur is essentially complete. The rest of the day will be spent elaborating on the theme, but we can joyously declare *She-Hecheyanu* with the knowledge that our forgiveness is assured. We have already completed the "*na'aseh*"; and from this point on, until the final sounding of the shofar at the completion of *ne'ilah*, we will focus upon "*nishma*", deepening our appreciation of the gifts of *teshuva* and forgiveness that *Hashem* has granted us.

Rambam (*Hilchot Teshuvah* 7:6) describes the process of *teshuva* succinctly: "Yesterday he was despised… today he is loved." Before, he was one of the "*avaryanim*;" now, "*Salachti ke-devarecha*." This is indeed the best time for *She-Hecheyanu*, a celebration of our forgiveness as we begin to contemplate it further, to appreciate the *Torah She-Be'al Peh*, and to understand the unnatural state of the *bayit be'churbano*.

May we all feel the joy of *kappara* that comes with true *teshuva* as we contemplate the lessons of the Yom Kippur *machzor*.

Four Aspects
Requiring *Chizuk*

─────────── ❧❧ ───────────

THE *GEMARA* (*BERACHOT* 32B) TELLS us that there are four aspects of one's life that require "*chizuk*" (reinforcement, support, strengthening) – Torah, good deeds, prayer and *derech eretz*. Rashi explains that it is imperative that one invest all of one's energies in these four realms; their achievement demands effort and exertion. In this context, Rashi explains, "*derech eretz*" refers to one's vocation; the craftsman, merchant, and warrior must all exert themselves to accomplish their goals outside of their Torah lives as well.

Thus, the *gemara* essentially tells us that every aspect of one's life demands "*chizuk*." The categories of Torah, *mitzvot*, *davening*, and one's professional endeavors certainly seem to encompass every aspect of one's life! If everything we do in our spiritual and mundane lives requires *chizuk*, what is the point of the *gemara's* formulation?

The *gemara* continues to cite textual support for its assertion:

> From where do we know this regarding Torah and good deeds? As it says, "Only strengthen and fortify yourself much to observe all of the Torah" (*Yehoshua* 1:7). Strengthen yourself – in Torah. And fortify yourself – in good deeds.

Chazal use the double language in the verse to teach that both Torah and good deeds require "*chizuk.*"

The *gemara* goes on to cite a verse that indicates this requirement for prayer:

> From where do we know this regarding prayer? As it says, "Hope unto God; strengthen and fortify your heart and hope unto God" (*Tehillim 27:14*).

This verse clearly refers to prayer to God and explicitly states that "*chizuk*" is necessary.

Finally, the *gemara* cites a verse demonstrating the need for "*chizuk*" in the realm of *derech eretz*:

> From where do we know this regarding *derech eretz*? As it says, "Be strong and let us strengthen ourselves on behalf of our nation" (*Shmuel II* 10:12).

In the context of an upcoming battle, King David's general, Yoav, spoke these words of encouragement; the soldiers must strengthen themselves to do their part, and God will do as He sees fit.

Why do these four particular elements – Torah, good deeds, prayer, and vocation – demand "*chizuk*"?

❧ STRENGTHEN AND FORTIFY YOURSELF MUCH TO OBSERVE ALL OF THE TORAH

On the most elementary level, it is clear that Torah study requires exertion and effort. In fact, *Chazal* tell us that one must "kill" himself in the tents of Torah; extreme effort is required. This need is reflected in the words we say whenever we complete one of the books of the Torah, "*chazak chazak ve-nitchazek.*"[9] But what exactly is this "*chizuk*" that the *gemara* prescribes and that we offer ourselves upon engaging in Torah study?

Rav Soloveitchik further noted that in support of the notion that Torah study demands "*chizuk,*" the *gemara* chose to cite a verse from *Sefer Yehoshua*, even though there was an appropriate verse available from the Torah itself. Before Moshe's death, *Hashem* tells him, "Command Yehoshua and strengthen and fortify him (*chazkehu ve-amtzehu*)" (*Devarim* 3:28). Why didn't the *gemara* cite that verse as its source?

The Rav explained that the chosen verse is more significant because it was said by *Hashem* to Yehoshua after the death of Moshe Rabbeinu. Indeed, the first chapter of *Sefer Yehoshua* opens with the words, "*Moshe avdi meit,*" "Moshe my servant has died." Obviously, *Hashem* was not informing Yehoshua

---

9 Rav Soloveitchik suggested that according to the original practice, the congregation would recite the final verse of the book out loud, followed by the *ba'al korei*, just as we do when we read *Megillat Esther* and during some special Torah readings during the year. The Rav speculated that the word "*chazak*" printed at the end of each *sefer* was actually the initials of "*chazzan kahal,*" instructing how this final verse was to be read. The Rav admitted, however, that this was his own theory and that he knew of no sources reflecting this conclusion.

of Moshe's death, but was rather helping Yehoshua address a great crisis confronting him and the entire Jewish People. Upon Moshe's death, *Chazal* tell us, 3,000 *halachot* were forgotten. Yehoshua realized that he was no Moshe; filling his predecessor's shoes would be no easy task. *Am Yisrael*, in their grief, likely felt that all was lost. No one could possibly replace their leader. How could they carry on without him?[10]

Hashem turned to Yehoshua and told him, "*Moshe avdi meit*" – it is true that the singular and unique individual, Moshe, is no longer alive, but the story of Am Yisrael does not end with him. "Strengthen and fortify yourself much" – *Hashem* needed to strengthen Yehoshua to fill the shoes that he considered too big for him.

Yehoshua was faced with another challenge as well. On the one hand, he was to be the leader of the nation, who would lead them in battle against their enemies and conquer and divide up the land. He had the gargantuan task of building the country from scratch. On the other hand, it was his responsibility to perpetuate the teaching and learning of the Torah – "*ve-hagita bo yomam valayla*" (*Yehoshua* 1:8). How can the two coexist? Even in stable times, it is difficult to balance these two aspects of life; how was Yehoshua

---

10 The *gemara* relates that some Jews had a similar reaction following the destruction of the *Beit Ha-Mikdash*, separating themselves from meat and wine and all bodily pleasure. Without the *Beit Ha-Mikdash*, they insisted, how could they possibly go on living? In fact, *Chazal* relate that this reaction of utter helplessness was also found in the earliest days of the nation, when they were still enslaved in Egypt. Despondent as a result of the oppression, many Jews, led by Amram, separated from their wives. What was the point in raising families that would be obliterated by the Egyptians? Only Miriam was able to convince her father that he was making a mistake, after which he remarried Yocheved and Moshe was born.

supposed to maintain the Torah and its study while involved in intricate affairs of state? Yehoshua was involved in the conquest of *Eretz Yisrael* for the remainder of his life. How was this conquest going to coexist with his commitment to Torah study?

Indeed, the Rav noted, in *Sefer Devarim*, Moshe was commanded to encourage and strengthen Yehoshua specifically in his role as leader, the one who would lead the people in war and conquest. In the verse in *Yehoshua*, by contrast, *Hashem* encourages Yehoshua to be strong in his observance of the Torah. *Hashem*'s message was clear: You may believe you cannot do both – but you can! You think that you are incapable – but you are wrong!

In modern times, many of us are faced with the same question. Can a life dedicated to intense Torah study go hand-in-hand with a life spent at the work place? Doesn't the choice of one path necessitate the rejection of the other? The answer is that we are commanded and have the capability to do both. We are not expected to reach the achievements of Moshe or Yehoshua. As the old Chassidishe *vort* reminds us - in the *Olam Ha-Emet*, *Hashem* will not ask Reuven why he was not Moshe Rabbeinu, but rather why he did not actualize the potential of Reuven. By actualizing one's ability to balance his daily life with Torah study, he can reach his full potential.

Chazal tell us that Yehoshua was not even the greatest of Moshe's students; Pinchas was in fact far superior. Yeshoshua was chosen because when Moshe would enter his tent to teach the *zekeinim*, Yehoshua would enter first to set up the chairs. Yehoshua was a *ben bayit* of Moshe. He saw how Moshe lived his life. He was not only a product of the transmission of Torah learning, but also of devotion to Torah and *ma'asim tovim*. He was the keeper of the *masoret*, and that enabled him to persevere in spite of the difficulties.

We are responsible for taking on the role of *lomdei Torah* even when we think that we cannot accomplish all that is expected of us. Rav Yisrael Salanter used to say that it is our responsibility "*tzu tun*," to do, "*nisht tzu oftun*," not to accomplish. We must exert ourselves in learning Torah, even if we never finish the entire *Shas* or all of the commentaries of Ramban on the Torah.

A *cheshbon ha-nefesh* before Yom Kippur must include a reassessment of what our capabilities truly are – not what we've convinced ourselves that they are. Everyone has found their own "comfort-zone" when it comes to Torah and *mitzvot*. Instead of choosing not to do things that are "not me," one must reevaluate exactly who "me" really is. In spite of all of our responsibilities – our professions, our families, and our distractions – *Hashem* tells us that it is our responsibility to invest all of our energies into doing what we can. "Only strengthen and fortify yourself much to observe all of the Torah" – Torah and *ma'asim tovim* are within our reach, but require constant *chizuk* to remind us of our capabilities.

❧ HOPE TO GOD; STRENGTHEN AND FORTIFY YOUR HEART AND HOPE TO GOD

Interestingly, although *tefillah*, prayer, might well be included in the category of *ma'asim tovim*, the *gemara* chose to differentiate between the two. The problem posed by prayer is essentially different, and the *chizuk* required is therefore also different. The problem of *tefillah* is presented in the preceding lines in the *gemara*:

> If a person sees that he prayed and was not answered, he should pray again, as it says, "Hope to God; strengthen and fortify your heart and hope to God."

Sometimes, we invest energy in prayer – "Hope to God" – only to be disappointed, as we do not receive the answer we hoped for. The proper response, the verse tells us, is "strengthen and fortify your heart" – and then do it again, and perhaps even again and again.

The disappointment that may result from the expectations of an intense and meaningful *tefillah* can be severe. I vividly recall the mass prayer gathering at the *Kotel* when Nachshon Waxman was taken captive. The level of emotion and the greatness of the *tefillah* was unprecedented, with thousands of Jews pouring out their hearts to save an innocent Jewish soldier – who in the end was unfortunately not spared. More recently, before the Jewish communities were forcefully removed from the Gush Katif, Rav Mordechai Eliyahu Ztz"l stated regarding the intended expulsion - *"Hayo lo Tihya"*. He was later criticized for this statement, as it sounded like a declaration rather than a prayer, leading to a crisis of faith. But even if it was indeed a *tefillah* beseeching *Hashem* to rescind the *gezeirah*, why wasn't that sincere prayer, in addition to the prayers of thousands of Jews, answered positively? How can we continue with any meaningful *tefillah* when our efforts at prayer do not procure the response we desire? This challenge can lead to a true crisis in faith. Why should one be expected to exert effort when his prayers are not effective?

Rav Soloveitchik explained that *Chazal* make the point of telling us that this is not the response that *Hashem* wants. If our prayer doesn't achieve the desired result, we must remain devoted to it – "strengthen and fortify your heart and hope to God."

I would like to suggest another explanation based on an earlier statement of the *gemara (Berachot 32b)*:

> Anyone who prolongs his prayers – his prayers do not return unanswered. From where do we learn this? From Moshe Rabbeinu, as it says, "And I prayed to God," and it says afterward, "And God heard me that time as well." Is this so? Did not Rav Chiya bar Abba say in the name of Rav Yochanan: Anyone who prolongs his prayer and expects it to be answered (*me'ayen bah*) will in the end come to heartache, as it says, "Hope deferred makes the heart sick..." ... This is not a question. This [the latter] refers to one who prolongs his prayer and expects it to be answered; this [the former] refers to one who prolongs his prayer and does not expect it to be answered.

The *gemara* begins by suggesting that if one invests a great deal of time in his prayers and recites a lengthy *tefillah*, his prayers will be answered, just as Moshe Rabbeinu's forty-day long prayer on Har Sinai was answered and the Jewish People were forgiven for the *chet ha-egel*. The *gemara* then questions this based on another statement, which asserts that if one recites a lengthy prayer and is "*me'ayen bah*," he will eventually encounter "pain in his heart." Rashi explains that this person assumes that his prayers will be answered as a result of his lengthy *tefillah*. The *gemara* concludes that such a person, who expects his prayers to be answered, will surely experience disappointment and pain. One who simply exerts himself in *tefillah*, however, without expectation of the response he desires, will avoid that pain.

Tosafot elaborate on this idea. Our *gemara* implies that "*iyun tefillah*," the expectation that one's prayers will be answered, is undesirable. This is similarly indicated by another *gemara* (*Rosh Hashana* 16b) that states that *iyun tefillah* leads to *Hashem*'s judgment and assessment; does one really deserve that his prayers be answered? On the other hand, the famous *beraita* "*Eilu Devarim*" which we recite each morning lists "*iyun tefillah*" as one of the righteous acts whose fruits we enjoy in this world, while the true reward remains for the World to Come. Tosafot conclude that there are actually two types of *iyun tefillah*. One is the expectation that one's prayers will be answered; this *iyun tefillah* is viewed negatively. The positive "*iyun tefillah*," in contrast, refers to concentrating on one's prayers, focusing on one's words, rather than reciting them by rote. This type of *iyun tefillah* does not include any expectation that *Hashem* will actually respond.

Why did *Chazal* use the same term to refer to two different types of *tefillah*, one of which is viewed negatively while the other is viewed quite positively? In truth, the line between the two is extremely thin. After all, doesn't proper and sincere *kavana* in "*Refa'einu Hashem*" imply that one expects *Hashem* to heal the sick?

It is for this reason, I propose, that *tefillah* requires *chizuk*. We must be careful not to overstep that line. On the one hand, we must take heed that our *tefillah* not become a rote exercise, mere repetition of the words we have recited hundreds of times before, while at the same time thinking of other matters entirely. When one's *tefillah* is bereft of all true intent, this is not a case where *chizuk* is needed; in such a case, one must overhaul his entire attitude toward *tefillah*. Chizuk is necessary where one is concentrating on what he's saying – but while doing so, he must recognize that *Hashem* will ultimately do what is right in His eyes. That is the *chizuk* necessary for *tefillah*.

~ BE STRONG AND LET US STRENGTHEN OURSELVES ON BEHALF OF OUR NATION

The final category of necessary *chizuk* refers to all our mundane endeavors. Interestingly, the *gemara* does not quote the verse of *"chazkehu ve-amtzehu""* regarding Yeshoshua, who was commanded to strengthen himself to fight the wars of conquest. Those wars were *milchamot mitzvah*, and are therefore included in the category of *ma'asim tovim*. The war of Yoav and Avishai, although waged at the command of King David, was a *milchemet reshut* and therefore a "mundane" affair. This war serves as an example of virtually every endeavor we undertake in our everyday lives.

Often, despite our great efforts, success eludes us. I'm a good person, one might say. I daven, I learn, I give *tzedaka*. The least that *Hashem* might do is grant me success every once in a while! Why do we often fail despite our best efforts? Why do we experience health problems and child-raising problems and *shidduch* problems and financial problems?

Yoav went out to fight against Amon in a two-front war under difficult circumstances. Yet he did not say, "Let us strengthen ourselves, for success is assured!" Rather, he emphasized, "Be strong and let us strengthen ourselves on behalf of our nation" – we have to do our part, but then *Hashem* will do what is right in His eyes. Our job is to make sure that we've done everything in our power to assure success; the rest is up to *Hashem*'s will. There is no guarantee that *Hashem* will respond as we had hoped.

This attitude demands *chizuk*. This level of *bitachon*, where we are certain that *Hashem* will help us but are willing to accept that He may not in fact help us in the manner that we wished and prayed for, is a high level indeed. At this level, one accepts the *ratzon Hashem* and no feeling of hopelessness impedes one from moving on.

"Be strong and let us strengthen ourselves on behalf of our nation" – one's intentions must be focused on the right goal. Faced with amazingly difficult challenges on a national level, we must sometimes make decisions – and they are not always right. We have no choice but to do what we have to do, to act. And if we act "on behalf of our nation and behalf of the cities of our God," instead of on behalf of our politics or constituency, then at least we can rest assured that we've done what we had to do, despite the disappointments and failures. Sometimes, defeat is part of the *ratzon Hashem* – and then we must pick up the pieces and act again. The *gemara* tells us that the resistance to giving up in the face of adversity requires *chizuk*.

As we perform our *cheshbon ha-nefesh* before Yom Kippur, let us take the opportunity to give ourselves *chizuk* in each of these areas. May we realize that we are greater than we thought we were, that our capabilities in the realms of Torah and *ma'asim tovim* are worth reaching for, despite the distractions. May we be able to talk to *Hashem* without demanding of Him and to pick up the pieces after disappointment so that we can formulate a positive attitude towards life. In this way, we will be able to stand before *Hashem* with a clean heart, having made peace with the challenges we encounter, having developed a plan of action, and having found our true place in all four realms.

Overcoming the
Akeida

─────────── ৵৯৶ ───────────

The period of the *Yamim Nora'im* is the conclusion and beginning of the annual cycle of *cheit* and *teshuvah*. We accumulate many sins during the year; Elul, Rosh Hashana, and the *Aseret Yemei Teshuva* bring the necessary *hit'orerut* to repent, reaching a peak at Yom Kippur. When we leave *shul* after *Ne'ila*, cleansed of our sins and with a new lease on life, we begin the next year. And a year later, we repeat the process once again…

It is a fact of human nature that despite the new beginnings that we are offered, we never maximize the potential of those new beginnings. Each year, we find ourselves performing a *cheshbon ha-nefesh*, begging for forgiveness, and recognizing our inability to make commitments that will last more than

– at most – a year. The Torah clearly takes this aspect of our humanity into account, as it establishes this annual meeting between us and *Ha-Kadosh Baruch Hu.*

In addition to the cycle of sin and repentance, the *Yamim Nora'im* also mark a cycle of a different sort – the cycle of meta-human events of the Creation and *Matan Torah.* Thus, Rosh Hashana is declared, "*Zeh ha-yom techilat ma'asecha,*" the commemoration of the beginning of Creation; it represents the day of *bri'at ha-olam.* Similarly, in *Zichronot* we recall the awesome events that took place at the giving of the Torah. We remind ourselves – and *Ha-Kadosh Baruch Hu,* as it were – of the super-human *mesirut nefesh* of Avraham Avinu at the *akeida,* using this event as a springboard for asking *Hashem* to have *rachmanut* on the world, even if we ourselves are not worthy. These events are essentially beyond our comprehension, but we remind ourselves of them in the hope of arousing both ourselves and *Ha-Kadosh Baruch Hu.*

A third cycle of the *Yamim Nora'im* is that of coping – coping with the daily events of our personal lives. Throughout the year, we are forced to deal with difficulties, challenges, and tragedies, many of which are not of our own making. The unexpected and sometimes unbearable events we experience almost inevitably lead us to the famous question of why bad things happen to good people, why we suffer when we don't seem to deserve it at all. We are forced to face the terrifying question of "*Mi yichyeh u-mi yamut... mi ba-ra'ash u-mi ba-magefa,*" but significantly, we do not ask, "*Mi yisulach u-mi yitkaper.*" When we begin to view the *Yamim Nora'im* as the beginning of our annual cycle of coping with this reality, the entire time period takes on a different meaning.

ᔛ SARAH IMEINU AND THE *AKEIDA*

The story of the *akeida* is a prominent one throughout the period of the *Yamim Nora'im*. We mention it repeatedly in the hope that Avraham's willingness to sacrifice his son will serve as *zechut avot* that will stand in our stead. We blow the *shofar*, representing the horn of the ram sacrificed in Yitzchak's place, to further remind *Hashem* of the *akeida*. At first glance, the focus is upon Avraham's role in this story, but in fact, there are three different characters involved – Avraham, Yitzchak, and Sarah – and each plays a different role in the significance of the *akeida* in the *Yamim Nora'im* liturgy.

On the first day of Rosh Hashana we read in the Torah the story of - "*Ve-Hashem pakad et Sarah*." Many suggest that this reading was chosen because it represents the birth of the Jewish People through Yitzchak's miraculous birth; Rosh Hashana should similarly mark a miraculous beginning and a promise of continuity for the Jewish People. I would suggest, however, that we read this selection on the first day – before the story of the *akeida*, which we read on the second day – in order to emphasize Sarah's role in the story. It is actually her response to the *akeida*, no less than Avraham's super-human *mesirut nefesh*, that *Chazal* wished to stress on Rosh Hashana.

Commenting on the *pasuk* of *Parshat Chayei Sarah* – "*Va-tamat Sarah be-Kiryat Arba*" – Rashi explains why this story is recorded immediately following the account of the *akeida* at the end of *Parshat Vayeira*:

> Sarah's death was juxtaposed to *akeidat Yitzchak*
> because it was a result of hearing the news of the

akeida – that her son was prepared for the slaughter and he was almost killed (*kim'at she-lo nishchat*) – that her soul departed from her and she died.

This comment raises a number of questions, among them the strange formulation of "*kimat she-lo nishchat*," which would be translated literally as "he was almost not killed." Furthermore, it seems somewhat strange that Sarah died from shock that her son was spared. If your child ran into the street in front of a moving car and was saved at the last minute, you would likely *bentch gomel* and suffer from some trauma, but it is unlikely you would die from the experience. Why was Sarah so affected by the news of the non-slaughter of her son?

There are actually three different midrashic sources for Rashi's comment. *Pirkei De-Rabbi Eliezer* relates:

When Avraham returned from Har Ha-Moriah, Samael [the *Satan*] was angered, for he saw that he had not succeeded in fulfilling his desire to prevent Avraham Avinu's sacrifice. What did he do? He went and told Sarah. He said: Have you heard what is going on in the world? She said: I have not. He said to her: Avraham took Yitzchak his son and slaughtered him and offered him on the altar as an *olah*. Sarah went and cried three *yevavot* to parallel the three *tekiot,* and three *yellalot* to parallel the three *yevavot,* and her soul departed from her and she died.

According to this version of the story, the *Satan* had tried in vain to prevent Avraham Avinu from bringing Yitzchak to the altar, but Avraham had succeeded in overcoming all the obstacles placed in his way so that he could be *omed ba-nisayon*. As revenge, the *Satan* resolved to tell Sarah about what has taken place, but adding the lie that Yitzchak had actually been killed – thus explaining Sarah's reaction.

This version has much less of an impact, because Sarah's reaction is readily understandable. Upon hearing that her only son had been killed, she wailed and cried, dying from the anguish of her loss.

The *Midrash Aggadah* adds to the same theme:

> Why was the story of the death of Sarah juxtaposed to that of *akeidat Yitzchak*? Because when Avraham came from Har Ha-Moriah, he found that Sarah had died as a result of the words of the *Satan*. For this reason, we blow the *shofar* on Rosh Hashanah – so that Sarah's death will serve for them as a *kapara*, for the *terua* is the sound of sobbing and wailing.

It is clear that Rashi did not entirely accept the version of events presented by these *midrashim*. According to these accounts, the *Satan* lied to Sarah, informing her that Yitzchak had died when he was actually spared. Rashi, however, writes that Sarah's death was a response to the shock of hearing that her son had *almost* been killed. Perhaps, then, his source was the *Midrash Tanchuma*, which records a different version of the same story:

> When he [Avraham] sent his hand to take it [the knife], a *bat kol* emanated and commanded from Heaven: Do not send your hand against the lad! And had this not taken place, he would already have been killed. At that very moment, the *Satan* went to Sarah in the guise of Yitzchak. When she saw him,

she said to him: My son, what did your father do to
you. He said to her: My father took me and brought
me up to the mountains and down to the valleys,
and he brought me to the top of one mountain and
built an altar and prepared the pile and ordered the
wood and tied me to the altar and took a knife to
slaughter me. And had *Ha-Kadosh Baruch Hu* not
declared, "Do not send your hand against the lad,"
I would already have been killed. He did not finish
the story before her soul departed.

According to this version, *Satan* told no lies to Sarah, but
rather presented a dramatic rendition of what took place,
apparently appearing before her as a disheveled and distraught
vision of her son. When his mother asked what had happened
to him, Yitzchak related the abuse that Avraham had put him
through, stressing that only *Hashem*'s intervention at the last
minute had saved his life. Yet even though Sarah sees whom
she believed to be "Yitzchak" with her very own eyes and
knows that he has survived, she cannot even manage to hear
him out before she dies of shock.

A third version of the story is similar to the second, but
with one important nuance. *Vayikra Rabba* relates:

He took the knife to slaughter him, and had it
not been for the fact that an angel called out to him
from heaven, he would already have been killed.
Know that this is true, for when Yitzchak returned
to his mother, she said to him: Where were you,
my son? He said to her: My father took me and
brought me up to the mountains and down to
the valleys... She declared: Woe to the son of the

drunken woman! [Is it then true that] were it not for the angel, you would have been slaughtered? He said to her: Yes. At that moment, she cried out six *kolot*, paralleling the six *tekiot*, and he did not finish the account before her soul departed and she died.

In this version, *Satan* makes no appearance at all! It is Yitzchak himself – the real Yitzchak – who relates to his mother what happened. There is no plot to affect Sarah's psyche, no plan to take revenge against Avraham by causing Sarah to die. Yitzchak simply explained what had happened, and his mother collapsed in shock. She declared that this news – that had it not been for the *malach*'s last minute intervention, her son would have been killed – was too much for her to bear.

Interestingly, all of these *midrashim* provide a different explanation for the blasts of the *shofar* on Rosh Hashana than the more commonly recognized explanation, relating to the *shofar* of the *ayil* ; it is the sound of Sarah's crying over her loss that the *kolot* recall.[11] Thus, the *shofar* not only reminds *Hashem* of the *mesirut nefesh* of Avraham Avinu; it also reminds Him of the first true victim of *akeidat Yitzchak* – Sarah Imeinu.

Rashi, *ke-darko ba-kodesh*, creates a composite of these midrashic comments in formulating his explanation of the *pasuk*. He does not mention what the source of the "*besurat ha-akeida*" was, in order to be consistent with all of the versions. What remains to be explained, however, is why Sarah died from her shock upon hearing that her son "*kimat*

---

11 Abudraham suggests a similar explanation.

she-lo nishchat," and certainly why she died if she actually saw her son in the flesh. Furthermore, this strange formulation demands an explanation.

Maharal explains in *Gur Aryeh* that it is part of human nature that upon hearing that someone dear to the listener was only a hairbreadth away from total disaster, he will panic, even to the extent that the trauma might be fatal. While this may provide some insight into Sarah's reaction, I think that it is an insufficient explanation. Instead, I believe that her response reflects something about her nature.

There are numerous examples that demonstrate that Sarah had a particularly clear vision of things; she appropriately evaluates the situations she faces and knows immediately how to respond. Thus, when she witnesses Yishmael "playing" inappropriately with Yitzchak – perhaps playing a bow and arrow version of Russian roulette, and perhaps involving himself with the three cardinal sins – she knows exactly what must be done: Yishmael has to go. While Avraham objects to her hasty response, *Hashem* ultimately concurs with her evaluation: *"Kol asher tomar eilecha Sarah shema be-kola."* Sarah is right; things will not work out if Yishmael remains.

After Sarah was taken by Avimelech, *Hashem* appeared to the king and compelled him to release her. When he did so the next morning, lavishing gifts upon Avraham, Avraham subsequently prays for Avimelech's recovery. According to Ramban, Sarah was quite displeased with Avraham's willingness to forgive Avimelech so easily. After all, the man had almost – but not quite – touched her. Who knows what he would have done had God not intervened!

Sarah's logical way of thinking is also reflected in her

response to the news that she would have a child at the age of 100. These things simply don't happen. In Sarah's mind, precautions must be taken in order to prevent evil, and logic must be used to evaluate the possibility of a good event. One must be an *oved Hashem* while still acting in a normal, human, logical manner.

Chazal often speak of the *Avot* as paradigms, archetypes of certain *middot* that blend together to form the Jewish People.[12] Avraham represents *chesed*; Yitzchak is *gevura*; Yaakov is *tiferet*. Sarah's central trait is the quest for logic in life, and that is the trait that informs her reaction to hearing the story of the *akeida* – whether it was the *Satan*, an impersonator of Yitzchak, or even Yitzchak himself who related it.

The story that Sarah hears is the very antithesis of her approach to serving *Hashem*. What Avraham did – because *Hashem* demanded it of him – was to take his son, tie him to the altar, and take a knife to slaughter him. He was about to kill his only son, the son after whom there would be no others; and were it not for *Hashem*'s intervention, he would have done it. Sarah, the paradigm of logic in *avodat Hashem*, simply could not comprehend this. She could not cope with God's demand to suspend logic altogether.

And so, she wailed and cried and ultimately died. On Rosh Hashana, we blow the *shofar* to remind ourselves of her sacrifice – and to remind God that sometimes we, like Sarah

---

12 Rav Soloveitchik talks about this at length in *Yemei Zikaron* in the context of the specific personalities of each of the *shevatim*. The twelve tribes blended together to form *Am Yisrael*, a nation that had all of the best that each of the *shevatim* had to offer.

Imeinu, simply cannot cope. A year has transpired, and many difficult, tragic things have happened – and sometimes, we find it exceedingly difficult to go on. When we blow the *shofar* on Rosh Hashana, we remind ourselves of Sarah's lot, as we ask for renewed strength and blessing, to empower us to cope with a life that sometimes makes no sense.

↬ YITZCHAK AVINU AND THE *AKEIDA*

While the theme of the *akeida* appears in the *Selichot* leading up to Rosh Hashana and on the day of Rosh Hashana itself, it becomes increasingly prominent in the *Selichot* of the *Aseret Yemei Tesuvah* leading up to Yom Kippur. At that point, there appears each day a *piyut* termed an "*Akeida*", which is built on the theme of that event. On Yom Kippur itself, the *akeida* is emphasized in the *piyutim* of Mincha.

A fascinating *ma'amar Chazal* connects the story of Yitzchak with the theme of *kapara*. On the verse, "*Asher yeomer ha-yom be-har Hashem yeiro'eh*" (*Bereishit* 22:14), Rashi comments:

> The *midrash* relates: *Hashem* will see this *akeida* to forgive Yisrael every year and to save them from punishment, so that it will be said in all future generations: *Hashem* will see the mountain, the ashes of Yitzchak are gathered together on the altar and remain there for atonement.

What does this reference to the "ashes of Yitzchak" mean? After all, Yitzchak was spared, not sacrificed.[13] How can his

---

13 There is a view that "*afro shel Yitzchak*" actually mans "*afar shel akeidat*

"ashes" then serve as a *kapara* for *Am Yisrael*?

This concept of "*afroh shel Yitzchak*" is not simply a *midrashic* idea; it has halachic ramifications as well. The *gemara* in *Zevachim* (62a) questions how Ezra and the returnees from Bavel knew where to build the *mizbei'ach* when it came time to rebuild the *Beit Ha-Mikdash*. Such a determination requires the input of a *navi*, and this is in fact one reason we are unable to rebuild the *Beit Ha-Mikdash* today. One opinion cited by the *gemara* explains: "They saw the ashes of Yitzchak resting in that place." Somehow, these ashes had been preserved, and served as an indication of the proper location of the *mizbei'ach*.

Similarly, a passage in *Masechet Ta'anit* (16a) explains the possible reasons for the practice of placing ashes on everyone's head during a *ta'anit tzibur*:

> Rabbi Levi bar Chama and Rabbi Chanina disagreed as to the reason. One said: [As if to say:] Behold, we are considered before you like ashes. The other maintained: In order to remind Him of the ashes of Yitzchak.

Interestingly, we want *Hashem* to recall the "sacrifice" of Yitzchak in our merit, not Avraham's willingness to sacrifice him. But what can this possibly mean? Yitzchak's body was never burned! How could there be ashes remaining after the *akeida*?[14]

Yitzchak," meaning the ashes of the *ayil* that took Yitzchak's place.

14 According to *Pirkei De-Rabbi Eliezer* (30), Yitzchak had a "near-death" experience - Rabbi Yehuda says: When the sword reached his neck, Yitzchak's soul departed. When he heard the voice emanating from among the *keruvim* declaring, "Do not send your hand against the lad," his soul returned to his

I think it may be possible to explain this idea if we keep in mind that Yitzchak was likely aware of the role that his near-sacrifice played in his mother's death. This is certainly the case if it was actually he himself who relayed the story to Sarah.[15] Perhaps he had thought that she would be happy that he had survived, but he had not taken into account the agony that the account would cause her. Now, Yitzchak not only had to deal with his grief over his mother's death; he also had to cope with his share of the responsibility in causing it. For this reason, it took him longer than usual to mourn his mother, and he was comforted only when he brought Rivka into Sarah's tent. As far as Yitzchak was concerned, it was only then that Sarah's light was reignited and he could move on with his life. Until that point, Yitzchak coped with the reality of his mother's death by withdrawing from the world around him.[16]

I believe that the same idea is reflected in another famous

body. Yitzchak stood up on his feet, and he knew that this is how the dead will come back to life in the future. He then declared: *Baruch Atah Hashem mechayeh ha-meitim*! Blessed are you *Hashem* who resurrects the dead. While this explanation is certainly interesting, it still does not explain the ashes.

15 In fact, according to *Bereishit Rabbah*, while Yitzchak was lying on the altar and he assumed that he would die, he told Avraham not to tell Sarah what had transpired while she was standing on a rooftop, as she was liable to jump to her death in response.

16 Some would object to this type of characterization of the *Avot*. How can we possibly say that the likes of Sarah or Yitzchak couldn't cope? This is, however, the clear implication of these *ma'amrei Chazal*. In fact, it is not only the greatness of the *Avot* that makes them symbols for us, but also their human-ness. We can then say before *Ha-Kadosh Baruch Hu*: If those as great as Sarah or Yitzchak responded as they did, how can we be expected to do any better?

midrash. In explaining why Yitzchak went blind in his old age, Rashi (*Bereishit* 27:1) cites a view that he lost his sight due to the tears of the *malachim* that fell into his eyes as he lay upon the *mizbei'ach* at the *akeida*. Although this is a poignant *midrash*, it is very difficult to understand on the literal level. After all, *malachim* lack any physical form; how can they possibly have tears? Moreover, why should their "tears" make Yitzchak blind, and why only much later in his life?

I would suggest that when Yitzchak became old, he began to think back on his life and contemplate its central event – the *akeida*. He thought about the trauma of stretching his neck out under his father's knife, and he thought about the event's effect on his mother. And the "light of his eyes" went out.

Yitzchak did not die from the trauma of the *akeida*, as did his mother, but it remained a critical influence for the remainder of his life. *Chazal* refer to "*pachad Yitzchak*;" he lived his life in the shadow of the *akeida*. Figuratively speaking, a part of Yitzchak actually did "die" on the *mizbei'ach*. A part of his otherwise healthy personality was forever burdened as a result of his experience – and that is *afroh shel Yitzchak*. Yitzchak's ashes represent the price he paid for the trauma of the *akeida*.

On Yom Kippur, when we make our personal *cheshbon ha-nefesh* and think about our actions of the past year, we often have difficulty getting beyond the less than glorious record that we have accumulated, the less than perfect manner in which we have served *Hashem*. On Yom Kippur, we ask *Ha-Kadosh Baruch Hu* to help us shed our baggage, by giving us the strength to renew our lives, to overcome the trauma that we cannot overcome on our own. We mention Yitzchak and the *akeida* to remind *Hashem* that we need assistance in order to turn over a new leaf and build a new life. We ask that He remember the *afroh shel Yitzchak* – and the ashes of each and every one of us. Yom Kippur gives us the ability to overcome the feeling of being weighed down by the past and progress to a new level of *Avodas Hashem*.

The theme of Yitzchak's ashes serving as a *zechut* for us appears in a number of the *piyutim* we recite during the period of the *Yamim Nora'im*. Thus, on *erev* Rosh Hashanah, we implore: "*Ve-afroh tamid yeiro'eh lifanecha le-chabsam*" – Yitzchak's ashes should always appear before *Hashem* to cleanse us of our sins. Similarly, in *Mincha* of Yom Kippur, we ask: "*Tireihu ha-yom ke-saruf be-ulalo, she-yizkor akeidato ve-tachon imo*" – "View him today as if he had been burned, to recall the *akeida* and give grace to his mother."

❧ AVRAHAM AND THE *AKEIDA*

It is actually in our daily *tefillot* that we recall Avraham's role in the *akeida* story when we recite the *akeida* passage in the *Korbanot*.

Interestingly, although Avraham faithfully fulfills *Hashem*'s commands in the story of the *akeida*, *Chazal* elaborate that after the events were over, he did question what had taken place. Rashi (*Bereishit* 22:12) cites the following *midrash*:

Avraham said to Him: I will relate my claims before You. Yesterday You told me: "For through Yitzchak will you have seed." Then You went back and said:

"Take your son." Now, [after I was prepared to do this deed,] You say to me: "Do not send your hand against the lad."

Avraham essentially demands an explanation for *Hashem*'s contradictory and illogical pronouncements. Avraham's question is a fundamental one: *Ribbono shel Olam*! How can You demand of us to do contradictory things? One minute You say this, and the next minute You say the opposite! One minute you promise us an *eretz zavat chalav u-devash*, and the next You demand that we sacrifice thousands of our best for the sake of a piece of desert with no sign of *devash* or *chalav*! What is the logic of that?

Ha-Kadosh Baruch Hu said to him: I will not violate My covenant and the words that emanated from My lips I shall not change. When I told you: "Take your son, your beloved," the words that emanated from My lips I did not change. I did not tell you to sacrifice him, but rather to "bring him up." You did what I asked of you; now take him down.

Hashem's response to Avraham's challenge is on its face not particularly satisfying. After all, *Hashem* told Avraham to take Yitzchak to Har Ha-Moriah and "bring him up there as a sacrifice" – not exactly leaving much room open for interpretation! Although He never used the words "slaughter him," *Hashem*'s intention was abundantly clear.

At its root, *Hashem*'s response was: When I tell you to sacrifice your son, you will go forward and do so. If I tell you not to, then you won't. And if I promise that your son will be the father of a great nation, then he will be exactly that.

Avraham's response to *Hashem*'s non-answer is silence. Avraham grasped Hashem's will in a way that neither Sarah nor Yitzchak did – that being a true *oved Hashem* means asking questions, challenging *Ha-Kadosh Baruch Hu* for answers, but moving on when we don't get them. We put our questions behind us and find the inner strength to continue in spite of the contradictions, improving our *Avodat Hashem* regardless of the fact that we have no answers.

Rambam writes in *Hilchot Teshuva* (10:2):

One who serves *Hashem* out of love involves himself in Torah and *mitzvot* and the paths of wisdom not because of any material need or due to fear of evil and not in order to benefit, but he rather does the truth because it is the truth – and in the end the good will come. This level is a very high level, and not all wise people merit it. It is the level of Avraham Avinu, whom *Ha-Kadosh Baruch Hu* called "*ohavo*," he who loves Me, for he only served Him out of love. This is the level that *Ha-Kadosh Baruch Hu* demanded of us through Moshe Rabbeinu when He said: "*Ve-ahavta et Hashem Elokecha*," "You shall love *Hashem* your God." And when a person loves *Hashem* to the appropriate degree, he will immediately perform all of the *mitzvot* out of love. And what is the appropriate degree of love? It is that he should love *Hashem* a great and awesome love to such a degree that his soul is bound with his love of *Hashem* and he is found enthralled in it at all time, as though he is lovesick. [Just as in the case of one who is lovesick,] his mind never departs from thoughts of his love for that particular woman and he thinks about her always, whether he is sitting or standing, or whether he is eating and drinking – more than that should be the love of *Hashem* in the hearts of all those who love Him, and they think about that lover always, as we are commanded: "With all of your heart and with all of your soul." And this was what Shlomo said by way of a *mashal*: "For I am lovesick." And all of *Shir Ha-Shirim* is a *mashal* for this idea.

Avraham Avinu is the epitome of *ahavat Hashem*, whose approach to *avodat Hashem* overcame the difficulties faced so tragically by Sarah and Yitzchak. This is why we repeat the story of the *akeida* each morning in our *tefillot*, from the perspective of Avraham – in order to help find within us the strength that will give us the ability to cope as *ovdei Hashem* – to ask the right questions, to sometimes find the answers, and to overcome the tendency to freeze in inaction when life is illogical and unexplainable.

On Rosh Hashana, we ask to be given the strength to continue, as Avraham did. On Yom Kippur, we ask that *Ha-Kadosh Baruch Hu* give us the strength to overcome the baggage of our past so that we not suffer the paralysis of *pachad Yitzchak*. And the morning after Yom Kippur, the morning we wake up to the beginning of a new year, we say, "*Va-yehi achar ha-devarim ha-eileh, va-Elokim nisa et Avraham.*" We set out on our lives again, and we hope and pray that *Ha-Kadosh Baruch Hu* will give us the strength to cope with life as *ovdei Hashem*, just as Avraham did.

Yissurim Memarkin

—————— ❧◦❧ ——————

The *gemara* in *Yoma* (86a) explains that there are four categories of sin, each requiring that the sinner undergo the *teshuva* process – including the stages of regret (*charata*), confession (*viduy*), and acceptance not to sin again (*kabbala al ha-atid*) – but some forms of sin demand more:

> If one transgressed a positive commandment and repented, he does not move from there until he is forgiven, as it is stated, "Return, O wayward children." If one transgressed a negative commandment and repented, the repentance suspends punishment and Yom Kippur atones for the sin, as it is stated, "For on this day He shall atone for you… from all your sins." If he committed sins

that are punishable by *karet* or by judicial execution, repentance and Yom Kippur suspend, and suffering purges the sin (*mimarkin*), as it is stated, "Then I will punish their transgression with the rod, and their iniquity with plagues." But as for one who bears the sin of desecration of the Name, repentance does not have the capacity to suspend punishment, nor Yom Kippur to atone, nor suffering to purge. Rather all of them suspend, and death purges the sin...

For one who failed to fulfill a *mitzvat asei*, who neglected to perform a deed he should have performed, *teshuva* is immediately successful upon recognition of the sin of omission. If he regrets failing to recite *kriat shema*, his *kapara* is immediate; if he feels remorse for having ignored the pleas of a poor person knocking at his door and resolves not to do it again, the *teshuva* process is complete. The blemish is erased from his record without any further ado.[17]

If one violated a *mitzvat lo ta'asei*, however, the process is a bit more complex. The deed is already done and the metaphysical scar has already been inflicted; *teshuva* is not enough to erase the effect. A new reality has been created, and no amount of regret can change it. In addition to *teshuva*, the day of Yom Kippur – the power of the *itzumo shel yom* – is necessary.

In the case of more severe sins – those liable for punishment

---

17 Indeed, Halacha recognizes the possibility of instantaneous conversion from *rasha* to *tzadik* in accepting the *kiddushin* of one who declares that he is *mekadesh* a woman on the condition that he is a *tzadik* even if it is known that he is not. A person has the ability to transform himself in a single moment.

by *karet* and *mitat beit din* – even the power of Yom Kippur is insufficient to affect complete *kapara*. "*Yissurim*" are necessary as well.

Finally, if a sin entails a *chilul Hashem*, desecration of *Hashem's* name, even *yissurim* cannot help; only death can completely erase the sin.

❧ YISSURIM MIMARKIN

I would like to focus on the third category of repentance noted by the *gemara* – *kapara* for sins that demands "*yissurim*." What kind of "suffering" is the *gemara* referring to here? What kind of *yissurim* are necessary in order to "purge" one's severe sins?

The *gemara* discusses the concept of *yissurim* elsewhere (*Berachot* 5a), but there the concept is clearly different in nature. The idea that Torah, *Eretz Yisrael*, and *Olam Ha-Ba* can only be acquired through *yissurim* is clearly different than the notion that *yissurim* may serve as a repair for sin. Furthermore, the *yissurim* under discussion are not the "*yissurim shel ahava*" described by the *gemara* in *Berachot*, which are not responses to sin. What, then, are the *yissurim* that the *gemara* intends in describing how suffering can "purge" one of sin?

Rav Soloveitchik explains that the answer can be found in a *gemara* in *Erchin* (16b) that describes the minimum degree of suffering that can be viewed as divine punishment for one's sins:

How far does the definition of suffering extend?

Rav Elazar said: For example, whoever has a

garment woven for him to wear but it does not fit him properly… But they said more than that! For example, even if they intended to mix [wine] in hot [water], but instead they mixed it in cold for him… Even if his shirt was reversed… Even if one extended his hand into a purse to take out three coins and only two came up in his hand.

The type of *yissurim* that purge one of his most severe sins – those for which he is liable for *karet* and *mitat beit din* – is not the *yissurim* necessary to acquire *Eretz Yisrael*. We all know, unfortunately, that those *yissurim* are far, far more difficult. It is not *yissurim shel ahava*, which often entails deathly illness. It is rather the "*yissurim*" of getting ice coffee instead of a hot, steaming cup! A disappointment at the tailor is enough to bring *kapara* to someone who ate on Yom Kippur!

Rav Soloveitchik noted that this highlights an important idea that we see throughout Halacha – the power of something small to affect something great. If one separated *terumot* and *ma'asrot* from a pile of grain and one grain of *tevel* is accidentally mixed in, the entire pile becomes inedible. "*Chita achat poselet*" – even a miniscule quantity has a profound effect. Similarly, a *kinyan*, formal transfer of ownership, can be accomplished through the transfer of a single *peruta*; in a *kinyan chalifin*, it can be affected by the transfer of a completely valueless object.

In the same way, Rav Soloveitchik explains, *Hashem* accepts the "suffering" of a misplaced coin or a badly tailored suit as a symbolic *tikkun*. *Hashem* gave us everything we have, and when we do *aveirot* and violate His will, we effectively throw His gift back at Him. Our lives were given to us on condition that we fulfill the Torah and *mitzvot*; by ignoring that condition, we have stolen our lives from *Hashem*. For this reason, we *daven* in *Ne'ilah*, "*lema'an nechdal mei-oshek yadeinu*," that we cease stealing. We pray that by desisting from sin, we no longer will wrongfully steal our lives from God. To buy back our rights to life and happiness, *Hashem* offers us a deal; we give Him a "*peruta*" – symbolic suffering – and He will grant us our lives. The "*yissurim*" at the tailor is not real suffering, but rather a reminder that *Hashem* is in charge. *Hashem* does not want us to suffer – He simply wishes to offer us a wake-up call.

❧ SACRIFICES TO THE SATAN

Rav Soloveitchik explains that there is a related form of suffering that can similarly assist us in achieving *kapara* for even the most severe of sins. In explaining the meaning of the ritual of the *se'ir la-azazel*, Ramban writes (*Vayikra* 16:8):

> For this reason they would offer Samael a bribe on Yom Kippur, so that he would not negate their sacrifice... Samael saw that no sins could be found on them on Yom Kippur. He would say before *Ha-Kadosh Baruch Hu*: Master of the World! You have one nation on earth who are like the ministering angels in heaven... *Ha-Kadosh Baruch Hu* would hear the testimony regarding Yisrael from their prosecutor, and He would grant *kapara* to the altar and the Temple and the priests and the entire nation...

We essentially "pay off" the Satan with the *se'ir la-azazel* so that he will argue in our defense before *Hashem* on the Day of Judgment. Although this idea seems quite radical – and perhaps even heretical –Ramban insists that we are not actually sacrificing anything to Samael. Rather, we are bringing a sacrifice to *Hashem*, who commands us to give it to the Satan, just as a master might command a caterer to offer food to his servant. If one were to offer the servant food without a command from the king, that would indeed be improper, but once the master commands it, it is entirely acceptable. A sacrifice to the servant – the Satan – is really a sacrifice to *Hashem*.

Rav Soloveitchik notes that throughout the year, we offer many *karbanot* to "Samael," sacrifices to values other than those of God. We expend time, energy, and money on things other than *kedusha*, which by definition are forces of evil. We sacrifice so much to achieve fleeting honor, excessive comforts, and elusive power. Indeed, we often suffer and agonize and lose for their sake, with little to show for our efforts. But God does a tremendous *chesed* for us; he credits us with the value of the suffering and anguish we endure for the sake of these unholy sacrifices[18] and counts them towards the suffering necessary to "purge" our sins. *Hashem* accepts our sacrifices to Satan, our *se'ir la-azazel*, even though we shouldn't have made them.

To bring complete *kapara*, *Hashem* demands only symbolic suffering – the petty *narishkeit* that gets us annoyed

---

18 Just as God recognizes the suffering endured when I seek three coins in my pocket and come up with only two, regardless of the purpose for which I sought out those coins.

under ordinary circumstances. In *Hashem*'s great mercy, the insults from our superiors, the annoyances from bureaucrats, as well as the suffering that we have endured at our own hands, are all sufficient to ensure *kapara*.

❧ UNTIL *YISSURIM* COME UPON HIM

Interestingly, when Rambam cites the *gemara*'s description of *kapara* through suffering (*Hilchot Teshuva* 1:4), he adds a line that seems redundant and unnecessary:

> If one violated a sin that is liable to *karet* or the *mitot beit din* and he did *teshuva*, his *teshuva* and Yom Kippur suspend, and *yissurim* come to him and complete the *kapara* for him. And he is never granted complete *kapara* until *yissurim* come upon him.

Why does Rambam add that one is "never granted complete *kapara* until *yissurim* come upon him"? What does this sentence add to the previous statement that *yissurim* complete the *kapara*?[19]

It seems that there is yet another form of suffering that qualifies as *yissurim* that can affect *kapara* – the psychological suffering that results from sin. This type of *yissurim* is described in the famous story recorded by the *gemara* in *Avoda Zara* (17a):

---

19 Rambam also does not quote the *gemara* directly, writing that *yissurim* "complete" the *kapara* (*gomrim alav et ha-teshuva*), nor that they "purge" one's sins (*memarkin et ha-cheit*). On the simplest level, this is because Rambam was concerned with writing a halachic work, not a philosophical or moral treatise; he did not wish to describe the metaphysical effect of *teshuva*, but rather the role of *yissurim* in the process.

They said about Rabbi Elazar ben Durdia that he did not leave over one harlot in the world without cohabiting with her. Once he heard that there was a harlot in one of the overseas cities who would take a purse of dinar coins as her fee. He took a purse of dinar coins and went and crossed seven rivers for her sake. At the moment of cohabitation, she blew with her mouth and said, "Just as this current of air cannot return to its place of origin, so they will not receive Elazar ben Durdia in repentance." Elazar went and sat between two mountains and foothills and he said, "Mountains and foothills, beseech mercy for me! … Heavens and earth, beseech mercy for me!... Sun and moon, beseech mercy for me!..." [When they did not help him,] he exclaimed, "*Ein ha-davar taluy elah bi*! The matter depends solely on me!" He placed his head between his knees and burst forth in crying until his soul departed from his body. A heavenly voice then issued forth and proclaimed, "Rabbi Elazar ben Durdia has now been readied for the life of the World to Come!"

I once heard Rav Amital *zt"l* explain that the *gemara* goes into such graphic detail about Rabbi Elazar's exploits because it was all part of his plan. He always intended to return to a proper way of life, but before reforming, he decided that he might as well get in as much pleasure as he could. Indeed, Rabbi Elazar clearly had tremendous inner strength, as he challenged all of nature to take up his cause. We can only imagine his great anguish when he realized that everything he had done in his life – including his project to enjoy as much as possible before changing his ways – was a colossal waste of time, energy, and potential. Here is a man who had powers that the mountains and stars lacked, and he had squandered them all.

Rabbi Elazar ben Durdia is the paradigm of *teshuva* because he was not only concerned with avoiding punishment, with achieving *mechila*. He wanted *selicha* as well, to be reinstated to his previous level of *kadosh, tahor,* and *naki.* This demands something more than the symbolic *yissurim* of petty annoyances or sacrifices; it entails the genuine anguish over wasted opportunities and one's previous pursuit of meaningless pastimes and pleasures. *Yissurim* "complete the *kapara* for him," but *teshuva* is not entirely finished until he experiences *yissurim* of the soul, suffering over what he wasted – "He is never granted complete *kapara* until *yissurim* come upon him."

It is the *teshuva* of *"ein ha-davar taluy elah bi,"* the realization that one is responsible for himself and that there are no excuses, that completes the *teshuva* process. It is the recognition that we have squandered the gifts of time, energy, and potential – and that we can blame no one but ourselves for our failures – that is the necessary *yissurim* that will assist us in achieving our desired *kapara* on Yom Kippur.

9/11 vs. 24/7

IN ISRAEL, WE ARE unfortunately well acquainted with sudden, tragic, and traumatic events that affect our psyche, both on the individual and national levels. For Americans, the prototype of such an event was 9/11 - a day of unexpected horror, a unique event that had a lasting impact on many people and upon the entire country. 9/11 is, in a sense, the very opposite of 24/7, the day to day, permanent, mundane events of life and history.

"9/11" type events often lead to *teshuva* transformations. In the aftermath of the Six Day War, for example, there was a tremendous outpouring of religious participation, a general feeling of inspiration and repentance, and the desire to connect on a national level. Major traumatic events arouse people to perform *cheshbon ha-nefesh*, to reassess their lives and their roles. Individual traumatic events are also often a trigger for repentance on a personal level. When a person suffers the death of a loved one, the sudden loss of employment, or a difficult illness, the common result is a reawakening, a reassessment and very often - significant change.

The concept of trauma as a source of repentance was certainly recognized by the great Jewish thinkers who discuss the idea of *teshuva*, but they do not emphasize its role. It would appear that they recognized that when *teshuva* results from trauma, it may very well be intense, but it is also likely to be short-lived; as soon as the initial arousal dissipates, the initiative to change does as well, and most people fall back into their previous "comfort zone". Indeed, this is exactly what happened in the years following the euphoria in the wake of the Six Day War. Thus, although Rambam mentions this type of *teshuva* in his discussion of repentance, he reserves it only for the later chapters, whereas the early chapters of *Hilchot Teshuva* address a more methodical process, not one of sudden, revolutionary change.

~ DAILY *TESHUVA* AND THE *TESHUVA* OF YOM KIPPUR

Interestingly, when Rambam introduces the concept of *teshuva*, he does not mention Yom Kippur at all. The process he describes is a response to sin any and every day of the year, an immediate reaction to one's realization that he must repent:

> All the commandments in the Torah, whether a positive or negative command – if a person

violated one of them, whether intentionally or
unintentionally, when he performs *teshuva* and
repents from his sin, he is obligated to confess before
God, may He be blessed... (*Hilchot Teshuva* 1:1)

The process of *teshuva* that Rambam describes involves
regretting one's sins, accepting that he will not do them
again, and verbally expressing *teshuva* through *viduy*,
confession, institutionalized in the *Ashamnu* and *Al Cheit*
prayers. Rambam does not here describe *teshuva* as involving
a revolution or sea change in a person's personality, but
rather, specific corrections that must be performed to fulfill
the *mitzva* of *teshuva*.

This *teshuva* has nothing to do with Yom Kippur. It is a
constant, even daily, process of recognizing one's sins and
committing to repentance. It is an immediate response to
sin: as soon as a person realizes that he has done an *aveira*, he
is obligated to do *teshuva*.

Chazal note that if one fails to perform a *mitzvat asei*,
a positive commandment, he is forgiven immediately and
completely as soon as he does *teshuva*. If he violated a *lav*,
however, although his *teshuva* is immediately accepted and
he will not be punished, complete *kapara* only takes place on
Yom Kippur. Nevertheless, the implication is that he need
not repent again on Yom Kippur. After all, he has already
undergone the entire *teshuva* process.[20] There is something

---

20 Similarly, for some very severe *aveirot*, even Yom Kippur is not sufficient to
affect repentance; one must also suffer *yissurim*. And if one is *mechalel shem
shamayim* in the process of sinning, even *yissurim* don't help; only the day of
death affects complete forgiveness. In all cases, however, *teshuva* is obligated
immediately.

about Yom Kippur that clearly contributes to the process of *teshuva*, even though that process is essentially performed daily. If *teshuva* is obligated and effective immediately, what is the purpose of Yom Kippur?

Rambam explains the purpose of Yom Kippur further in the next chapter of *Hilchot Teshuva*:

> Although repentance and prayer are always good for the world, during the ten days of repentance between *Rosh Hashana* and *Yom Kippur* it is even greater and it is accepted immediately, as it says, "*Dirshu Hashem be-himatzo*," "Seek out *Hashem* when He is found." (*Hilchot Teshuva* 2:6)

Although it is always appropriate, and indeed necessary, to do *teshuva* immediately, *Hashem* is closer to us during the *Aseret Yemei Teshuva*, and our *teshuva* therefore stands a better chance of being effective. The Chasidic masters used to say that during Elul, "*Yotzei ha-Melech la-sadeh*," the King is out in the field. The King, who is generally closeted inside His palace during the year, far from the populace, leaves those confines for a brief time and makes Himself accessible to all. While one should constantly regret his sins and reassess his life, *Hashem* makes Himself more available to us during this time period, and our *teshuva* is therefore more readily accepted.

Rambam limits this observation, however:

> About what is this said? In the case of an individual. But with regard to the community, they are answered any time that they do *teshuva* and call out with a complete heart, as it says, "*Ke-Hashem Elokeinu be-chol kor'einu eilav*," "Like Hashem our

God whenever we call out to Him." (*ibid.* 2:6)

Whereas an individual must wait for the special time of *teshuva* to have access to the "King," the *tzibur*, the community, has a "direct line" to *Hashem* whenever they call out to Him. Public prayer is just as effective in the middle of *Tevet* as in *Tishrei*, the *tzibur* need not wait for the *Aseret Yemei Teshuva*. The power of the *tzibur* lies in "*be-chol kor'einu eilav*," not in "*be-heyoto karov*."

Although this explains the importance of the Ten Days of Repentance, it does not address the special role of Yom Kippur itself. This is discussed in the next *halacha*:

> Yom Kippur is the time of repentance for everyone, individual and community, and it is the time of atonement and forgiveness for Israel. Therefore, everyone is obligated to repent and to confess on Yom Kippur... (*ibid.*, 2:7)

Whereas the *Aseret Yemei Teshuva* are necessary only for the individual, Yom Kippur itself is the "*zman teshuva la-kol*," the day of repentance for everyone.

At this point, we appear to be faced with a contradiction. On the one hand, one must do *teshuva* as soon as he becomes aware of his sin; he cannot wait until Yom Kippur to repent. At the same time, Rambam tells us that absolutely everyone must repent on Yom Kippur. Why? If I already did *teshuva* for my sins, why do I have to do *teshuva* again now? Even if my complete *kapara* is dependent on Yom Kippur, it is the day itself, the *itzumo shel yom*, that affects forgiveness.[21]

---

21 In a famous *machloket* recorded in the *gemara* (Yoma 85b), Rebbi maintained that the *itzumo shel yom* is *mechaper* even in the absence of *teshuva*, while the *Chachamim* maintained that the *itzumo shel yom* is *mechaper* only in

Why must I actually repent again? Indeed, the implication of Rambam is that even a complete *tzadik* must repent on Yom Kippur. But what is the purpose of such *teshuva*?

The solution to this problem is hinted to in the next *halacha*:

> ...Sins that he confessed this Yom Kippur, he may confess again on another Yom Kippur, even though he still maintains his repentance, as it says, "*Ki pesha'ai ani eida ve-chatati negdi tamid*," "For my sins I will make known and my sin is before me always." (*Hilchot Teshuva* 2:8)

This statement is actually one opinion cited in a *machloket* recorded in the *gemara* (*Yoma* 86b). According to one view, if one confessed sins on this Yom Kippur, he should not confess them again on a subsequent Yom Kippur unless he repeated the sin. If one did not commit the sin again but recited the confession anyway, this opinion maintains, he is like "a dog returning to his vomit." Why is he bringing up the past again? Not only is such behavior uncalled for, it is repulsive! Rav Eliezer ben Yaakov disagrees, however, maintaining that re-confession is actually a good quality, as the *pasuk* itself tells us: "*Ve-chatati negdi tamid*," "My sin is before me always." Rambam clearly sides with the second opinion, ruling that it is perfectly legitimate to confess for previous sins again, even if one has not returned to those sins.[22]

---

conjunction with *teshuva*.

22 Although it is unclear from Rambam's language if such re-confession is obligatory or simply permitted, *Shulchan Aruch* (*Orach Chayim* 607:4) clearly rules that while one is permitted to confess again, he is not obligated

According to this view, Yom Kippur is transformed into something totally different. It is not a day on which we only recount current shortcomings that we need to fix now. There is no set time of year for that type of *teshuva*; it is a 24/7 obligation. During the year, when we are faced with sin, we must fix the problem right away and move on with our lives, and it is only if we failed to do *teshuva* in a timely fashion that Yom Kippur serves that function. The purpose of Yom Kippur is not only to repair current failings, but rather to confess previous *aveirot*, even if we have already done *teshuva*; it is about cumulative soul-searching of one's entire life.

Teshuva is classically described as God's gift to humanity. *Ha-Kadosh Baruch Hu*, who is not limited by the constraints of time, can allow us to erase the past, to create a new reality in which our sins never happened. Although this is illogical and impossible in human terms, God is gracious enough to allow it to happen for our sake. Nevertheless, in human terms, what was done can never be undone. *Aveirot* still exist; time is unidirectional. Even though the past is behind us, we must still do cumulative soul searching, a review of every event and action that made us who we are and led us to this very moment. In fact, according to some versions of *viduy*, the text of the confession includes, "*aval anachnu ve-avoteinu chatanu*," acknowledging the sins of our fathers in addition to our own! Historical soul-searching entails reassessment of our lives in total, everything that contributed to our personalities.

---

to do so.

☙ VE-CHATATI NEGDI TAMID – MY SIN IS BEFORE ME ALWAYS

Interestingly, to prove that one may re-confess on a subsequent Yom Kippur, Rambam quotes a verse that would seemingly indicate that one must confess on a daily basis: "*ve-chatati negdi tamid*." Why is this verse interpreted as referring to the *teshuva* of Yom Kippur, when on its face it would appear to refer to our constant and daily recognition of our past sins?

I believe the answer lies in the flip side of this same verse. The *sefer Me'or Va-Shemesh* (*Haftarat Shabbat Shuva, d"h Oh*) writes that as long as we carry around the baggage of *aveirot* that we have not properly addressed, we cannot achieve true *dveikut* to *Hashem*. As long as the sin remains, there is a block between us and *Ha-Kadosh Baruch Hu*. David Ha-Melech therefore bemoans his state: "*Ve-chatati negdi tamid!*" My sins separate between me and God. I am cursed with the constant burden of my past sins, which I cannot forget no matter how hard I try.

On the one hand, we are obligated to place our sins before us always. We cannot forget the unpleasant aspects of our lives. On the other hand, we cannot become obsessed with our mistakes. Such an attitude can only lead to depression and despair over one's personal failings, that may actually impair his ability to improve and make changes in his life. When a person compares himself to the person he had once hoped to be, he will likely realize that there is no small gap between his dreams and his reality. He may then resign himself to the *status quo*, thinking that there is no chance to achieve those goals, instead of resolving to improve and change. He is more likely to slide back into this *status quo* when he realizes that he has not achieved his aspirations. *Ve-chatati negdi tamid* – my sins are ever present in my mind, and they unfortunately bog me down.

To resolve this tension, we have been given the gift of Yom Kippur, a special time for general reflection regarding our lives, a day that involves a structured program, a controlled environment, that is designed to inspire and assist us in accomplishing this objective. Surrounded by people going through the same process of soul-searching, we can allow ourselves to think of our lives as a unitary whole, to compare where we are and where we hope to be. But when the *shofar* blows at the end of *Ne'ila*, we can put those thoughts aside, so that we don't wallow in self-pity. The structure of Yom Kippur allows us to move on without fear of paralysis. Only on Yom Kippur can we rethink our entire lives in order to affect complete *kapara*.

On Yom Kippur, my sins are "*negdi*," before me, not "*negdicha*," before God. The *teshuva* of Yom Kippur is an internal process. We don't have to ask for forgiveness, because it has already been granted. On Yom Kippur, we review our sins not for God's "benefit," but rather for ours – so that we will grow from the process.

This is one possible reason why we recite the blessing of *Selach Lanu* in the *shemona Esreh* of *Ma'ariv* immediately after Yom Kippur. We never seem to enjoy the luxury of being pristinely clean, not even for a moment! Why must we ask for forgiveness if we have just been cleansed of all of our sins? On Yom Kippur, we reassess everything about our lives – and we realize that there is a lot left to be done. We leave Yom Kippur with a feeling of rebirth, with our plans back on track, and we realize that there were so many wasted opportunities and failures to accomplish. This is the purest *Selach Lanu* of the year, because it is at this point that we acknowledge that we will no longer be complacent about many of the things we previously let slide.

Yom Kippur is not about "9/11" events, one-time episodes that get us to do *teshuva*. In those cases, change is not really part of our nature; the impetus for change is purely external. Yom Kippur is about 24/7 – the reappraisal and recommitment of every minute of our lives.

A Flood of Suffering

———— ❧ ————

THE *MIDRASH* TEACHES (*TANCHUMA, RE'EH* 3):
"*Mi-pi Elyon lo teitzei ha-ra'ot ve-ha-tov*" (*Eicha*
3:38) – Rabbi Avin said: At the time that Yisrael
stood before Har Sinai and *Hashem* gave them the
Torah – from that point on, anyone who sinned, *Ha-
Kadosh Baruch Hu* punished him [personally]. In the
past, if anyone sinned, the generation would pay for
his sin. Our Rabbis taught that in the generation of
the flood, there were many righteous people of the
likes of Noach, but the entire generation was wiped
out. During the generation of the dispersion, they
sinned and even the infants paid. When Yisrael stood
at Har Sinai and *Ha-Kadosh Baruch Hu* gave them
the *mitzvot,* He said: In the past, the generations
were punished for the sins of an individual; from

now on, the generation will not be punished for the sin of an individual. This is the meaning of "*Mi-pi Elyon lo tetzei ha-ra'ot ve-ha-tov.*"

Until the time of *Matan Torah*, the *midrash* explains, there was collective punishment; the entire generation would suffer as a result of the sins of an individual. Thus, although there were numerous *tzadikim* during the time of Noach, they were destroyed along with the entire generation, and only Noach was saved. Even though they themselves were not guilty of any sins, they were swept away by the waters of the *mabul*.

Indeed, we do not need the *midrash* to tell us that there are times when *tzadikim* suffer alongside sinners during periods of massive destruction, their individual righteousness affording no protection. But interestingly, this *midrash* posits that *Matan Torah* changed the manner in which *Hashem* runs the world. *Tzadikim* are no longer destroyed along with their generation. Once the Torah was given, every individual stands on his own merit. "*Mi-pi Elyon lo tetzei ha-ra'ot ve-ha-tov*" – good and evil are now entirely in the hands of each and every person.

The same idea is conveyed in *Parshat Ha'azinu*, where we read (*Devarim* 32:4), "*Ha-Tzur tamim po'alo, ki chol derachav mishpat.*" Rashi explains, "Even though He is powerful, when He brings punishment upon those who violate His will, He does not bring them in a flood, but rather with justice, for His deeds are perfect."

These sources give us pause when we hear of or experience major catastrophes, and even personal ones. When "bad things happen to good people," we confront an eternal question. How does this reflect *Hashem*'s perfect justice? When we watch an airplane crash into the side of the World Trade Center, as we watch the building crumble to the ground and know that thousands of innocent people will meet their untimely deaths as a result, who does not wonder how *Hashem* can punish the *tzadikim* along with others? How can we understand these events in light of "*Ha-Tzur tamim po'alo*"?

The answer seems to be found in the following verses in *Ha'azinu*. "*Ha la-Hashem tigmilu zot, am naval ve-lo chacham (Devarim* 32:6)." Rashi explains: "*Am naval* (a despicable nation) – for they have forgotten what has been done to them. *Ve-lo chacham* (and unwise) – to understand history, that He has in His power to do good or bad." *Am Yisrael* does not remember the past, and therefore does not learn its valuable lessons. The next verse emphasizes the need to remember: "*Zechor yemot olam, binu shenot dor va-dor.*"

Surprisingly, when Rashi presents the events that we should recall and learn from, he does not mention the major events of Jewish history – *Yetziat Mitzrayim* and *Matan Torah*, for example. Instead, he writes: "[Remember] the generation of Enosh, when the waters of the ocean flooded them, and the generation of the Flood." Why should we recall the flood at the time of Noach? After all, *Hashem* promised that He would never again bring another *mabul* upon the earth. If such a cataclysm can never recur, why must we remember it and learn its lessons?

Upon further study of *Hashem*'s promise, however, it becomes clear that He pledged only that He would never again destroy the world completely, that the natural cycles would never cease again. But there is another aspect of the *mabul* that can and has recurred – the idea of *shetef,* that entire groups of people may be washed away, even if they do not deserve the fate that befell them. That is the aspect of the *mabul* that we must remember and learn from. On the eve of the entry into *Eretz Yisrael,* at the very beginning of his concluding words to *Am Yisrael,* Moshe Rabbeinu reminds the nation that good people sometimes suffer. He provides no explanation of why this is so, but the fact that he posits it reminds us that the phenomenon is not an anomaly; *Hashem* has already informed us that it will happen.

Only *nevi'im* can explain why a particular disaster happens in a particular time and place. But even in the absence of *nevu'ah,* it should be clear to us from our sources that these things happen as part of *Hashem*'s ultimate plan. The *beit din shel mata,* the earthly court, can only mete out punishment on an individual basis; flesh and blood judges cannot hold one person accountable for the crimes of another. But divine justice differs from human justice. The *beit din shel ma'alah* takes into account historical processes on a much larger scale, and individuals sometimes suffer through no fault of their own.

Moshe Rabbeinu chose to convey this message at this particular juncture because the next stage in Jewish history would entail war, and there are few wars without victims or casualties. Perhaps in some cases *Hashem* had a *cheshbon* with each and every soldier who died in war, but that's not necessarily so. In the last 100 years alone, wars have destroyed the lives of millions of innocent victims. We have no way of knowing why the victims of Stalinist Russia and

Nazi Europe were killed - *ki lo machshivotai machshivotechem* (*Isaiah* 55:8) - but in retrospect, we do know that important historical processes were at work. One could even argue that the creation of the State of Israel was a result of these historical events, which created the environment that made its existence possible. Many innocent people died in order for that to come to pass, and yet, from a global perspective, one might discern that there was a plan.

The image of *shetef*, a flood of suffering, is very powerful. Punishment is like the *mayim rabbim adirim mishberei yam*, the great force of waters that wash everything away, the good along with the bad. Rashi uses a similar image in his explanation of *Hashem*'s declaration of his intention to destroy the world, "*Ketz kol basar ba lifanai*" (*Bereishit* 6:13). Rashi writes, "In every place that you find promiscuity and idolatry, *andralamusia* comes to the world and kills the good and the bad." *Andralamusia* – a powerful version of the idea of *shetef* – sweeps away the good along with the evil not only in the time of the flood, but at all times.

Yeshayahu Ha-Navi also uses this image in his criticism of the political leaders of his day. These leaders delude themselves into thinking that they were safe as a result of the alliances that they made with other nations (*Yeshayahu* 28:15): "For you have said, 'We made a covenant with death, and with the grave we have made a contract; *Shot shotef ki ya'avor*, when the great flood will come, it will not come upon us." These leaders thought that they are immune to death, that they will not be swallowed up by the flood that will follow. Yeshayahu, however, begs to differ (28:18): "And your covenant with death shall be released, and your contract with the grave will not be fulfilled; *shot shotef ki ya'avor*, when the great flood comes, you will be trampled by it."

The people understood that there are times when a "flood" comes and everything gets washed away, but they thought they had found a solution to protect them from that flood. Yeshayahu warned them, however, that their "protection" was nothing but a fantasy; only *avodat Hashem* – not political machinations – can save them.

In the weeks and months and even years after a great tragedy, it is still premature to attempt to determine the greater plan, to explain why so many innocent people must die. Nevertheless, we must believe that there is such a plan. In the meantime, such events are a wake-up call, reminding us that our goodness is not always sufficient protection against the terrible things that happen in this world – drive-by shootings or bombs in restaurants or planes flying into buildings.

❧ OUR UNIVERSAL MESSAGE

The World Trade Center disaster provides us with an additional wake-up call. Jews in both Israel and *Chutz La-Aretz* tend to have a rather insular perspective in relating to the world at large. This perspective is partially rooted in our religious upbringing, which stresses our special relationship with *Hashem* as the *Am Ha-Nivchar*. Because we believe that we have a special relationship with *Hashem* and a special mission to perform, we tend to focus on perfecting our own behavior and assume that what the rest of the world does is simply not our concern. Suddenly, many people realize that that may not be accurate. We no longer live in an insular part of the globe – we live in a global village, and the world is now a very small place. Events occurring at the farthest corner of the globe affect us; we are not as insulated as we may think we are.

The idea of responsibility for the world, and not just ourselves, is inherent in our *tefillot* on Rosh Hashanah. Although Rosh Hashanah is the first day of the *Aseret Yemei Teshuva*, very little of our *nusach* on that day relates to the theme of individual repentance. The primary focus of Rosh Hashanah, as opposed to Yom Kippur, is not sin or forgiveness, but rather destiny and fate. The *goral* of the individual takes a back seat, and in its place we find a plea for the fate of mankind: "*U-vechein tein pachdecha Hashem Elokeinu al kol ma'asecha.*" We do not ask *Hashem* to make "*amcha*" fear Him, but rather that He turn the hearts of all of His creations. "*Ve-eimatcha al kol mah she-barata*" – we do not ask that *Hashem* make "*bnei britcha*" follow Him in awe, but rather speak in universal terms. "*Ve-yira'ucha kol ha-ma'asim ve-yishtachavu lefonecha kol ha-beru'im ve-yei'asu kulam aguda echat la-asot ritzonecha be-levav shalem*" – all of humanity should be unified in their service of *Hashem*.

This universalist message is also found in a *tefillah* that we recite numerous times every day, in addition to Rosh Hashanah – the *Aleinu* prayer. There, we pray, "*Ve-yeidu kol yoshvei teivel ki lecha tichra kol berech tishava kol lashon,*" that all of the inhabitants of the earth will realize that they should serve *Hashem*. Indeed, all of the nations of the world stand in judgment by our side on Rosh Hashanah – "*Ve-al ha-medinot yei'amer ezo la-cherev ve-eizo la-shalom…*"

While Rosh Hashana looks outwards and is essentially

universal in nature, Yom Kippur emphasizes the theme of individual merit, justifying our role as a member of the *Am Ha-Nivchar.* We have corrected our ways in order to demonstrate that we deserve to be part of this select group. This process, however, does not conclude on Yom Kippur;[23] the culmination of the process begun on Rosh Hashana and continued on Yom Kippur takes place on Sukkot. On Sukkot, 70 *korbanot* were brought in the *Beit Ha-Mikdash,* and *Chazal* tell us that they parallel the 70 nations of the world. After we have perfected ourselves on Yom Kippur, we return to the original mission of the *Yamim Nora'im* – that it is our role to bring the message of *Hashem* to the entire world. It is only after we have finished representing the world before *Hashem* that we are entitled to the intimate feast of *Shemini Atzeret,* which is reserved only for us.

Concern for the rest of the world, feeling the pain of the suffering of other people, of other nations, should not mistakenly be considered as a matter for others to focus upon. When we stand before *Hashem* on Rosh Hashana and declare that He will decide on this day what will become of the nations of the world, we should do so with as much fear, trembling and tears as we experience when focusing upon our own individual futures. The world in its entirety is *Hashem*'s creation, and we must appreciate the value of all of humanity.

---

23 I once heard the suggestion that the mistaken idea that Yom Kippur marks the end of the process is the reason that we must say "*Slach Lanu*" in *Ma'ariv* immediately following Yom Kippur. When we hear the *shofar* blow, we not only breathe a sigh of relief and rush home to eat; we come to the faulty conclusion that we have completed the entire process.

This does not only mean that we should shed a tear for the thousands of innocent people murdered in the United States, our greatest ally. In fact, it's obvious that we must do so; anyone who does not cry for the loss of these innocents has to examine whether his heart is made of flesh or stone. Feeling ourselves to be part of the world means that it is incumbent upon us to understand that the destiny of the world is intertwined with the destiny of the Jewish People because we have a common destiny. At some point in time when the *ge'ulah sheleima* will come about, it will not just come to the Jews. The ultimate *ge'ulah* will not only entail the rebuilding of the *Beit Ha-Mikdash*; it will bring about the *tikkun* of the entire world. That new world will be one in which all the nations of the world accept *Hashem* as their God. In that world, there will be no more evil. All of the Bin Ladins of the world will simply disappear.

Twenty years ago, building *Eretz Yisrael* was still the primary purpose of our existence here. We certainly have not finished the job, unfortunately. But we no longer have the luxury to be interested only in ourselves. History is moving too quickly.

In *Hilchot Teshuva* (3:1-2,4), Rambam discusses three levels of accounting for merits and sins:

> Every individual of humanity has merits and sins. One whose merits are greater than his sins is deemed a *tzaddik*, and one whose sins are greater than his merits is deemed a *rasha*, and one who is 'half and half' is deemed a *beinoni*. The same is true of a country – if the merits of all of its inhabitants are greater than their sins, it is deemed righteous,

and if their sins are greater, it is deemed evil. And similarly the entire world. If an individual's sins are greater than his merits, he immediately dies in his evil… Similarly, if the sins of a country are greater, it is immediately destroyed… And similarly, if the sins of the entire world are greater than its merits, they are immediately obliterated, as it says, "And *Hashem* saw that the evil of man was great"[24]… Therefore, every person must view himself throughout the entire year as if he is half-meritorious and half-guilty, and similarly that the entire world is half-meritorious and half-guilty. If he commits one sin, he has weighed himself and the entire world towards the side of guilt and has caused its destruction; if he performs one *mitzvah*, he has weighed himself and the entire world towards the side of merit and has caused himself and them salvation and deliverance…

In these *halachot*, Rambam rules that in all of our actions, we have a responsibility not only to ourselves, but to the entire world as well. Our actions determine not only our own individual destiny, but the destiny of the entire world. Every individual has the responsibility to do what he can, not only for himself and his family and his community and his country, but for all of humanity. This is not simply a platitude; it is a *halacha*! That was wake-up call number two of September 11th.

---

24 The fact that the Rambam quotes a *pasuk* that relates to the *mabul* indicates that in his view, the *mabul* is still a very relevant message, as noted above.

There is a third wake-up call in these events as well. We all become used to the way things generally function and begin to take our lives for granted, as if nothing could possibly ever change. Perhaps this is less so in *Medinat Yisrael*, given the fact that our hold of the land seems so tentative due to the constant struggle we have endured over the years. But the Jews in the Diaspora today, especially in the West, on the other hand, have a sense that they have reached the end of history. They have convinced themselves that everything will be fine from here on in. This is not the same situation as the Jews in Spain before Ferdinand and Isabella. This is not the same situation as the Jews in Europe (or England, or Canada, etc.). before Nazi Germany. This is the United States of America. This is it. Here, we have arrived.[25]

The events of September 11th have put the lie to that claim. As we began to get a taste of the first war of the 21st century, it has become abundantly clear that history is far from over. We have simply moved on from a struggle against Communism and Fascism to a struggle against fanatical terrorism.

The feeling that we have arrived is not only prevalent

---

25 There was actually a trend at one point to view the fall of Communism and the rise of the United States as the major world power as the end of history. I recall attending a lecture in which Professor Harkavy essentially argued that now that the United States had vanquished all of its enemies, its culture will become paramount and eventually take over the world. History has reached its end. When a student asked what would happen when all of the millions of disenfranchised people in Africa and Asia would fight back and demand that they also benefit from these changes, Professor Harkavy laughed and said, "What will they do, throw spears at the United States?!" Well, they didn't throw spears; they threw airplanes.

in politics or global history; we experience it as individuals as well. Every person has carved out for himself a certain level of *kiyum ha-mitzvot* with which he feels comfortable, a certain amount of time that he's willing to dedicate to Torah study, to teaching Torah to his children, and to *tefillah*, and a certain amount of money that he's willing to give to *tzedaka*. Everyone has his own comfort level in his *avodat Hashem*, which he defines as his identity, how he views himself as an observant Jew.

The destruction of the World Trade Center was symbolic in a sense, as it shattered many of our beliefs about the world. Our confidence has been pulled out from under us. If such buildings can be destroyed, if airplanes can be hijacked with such apparent ease, if the intelligence community could be so failing in its ability to discover any hint that these things were going to happen, then what does that say about my personal security, about national security, and about the future in general? We can no longer feel that we have arrived anywhere. Our certainties have been entirely erased, and no new certainties have come to replace them as of yet.

There is, in fact, only one certainty in our lives, the certainty of "*tamim tihiyeh im Hashem Elokecha*." It is useless to predict the future, because the future will take turns that are so unexpected that we never could have dreamed that they would happen. *Temimut*, in contrast, means simply that we believe in the charity and the kindness and the justice of *Ha-Kadosh Baruch Hu*. That is all. Beyond that there are no certainties.

Hetiach Devarim
Kelapei Ma'alah

~~~~~~

THE OPENING *PASUK* OF the *haftara* of *Shabbat Shuva* introduces a simple equation: "*Shuva Yisrael ad Hashem Elokecha, ki kashalta ba-avonecha,*" "Return Israel to *Hashem* your God, for you have stumbled in your sin." One must do *teshuva* because he has failed; he has not lived up to God's expectations. This equation leaves no room for excuse, no chance of submitting an appeal for "mitigating circumstances." If you have sinned, you must do *teshuva*.

It is clear from *Chazal*, however, that the equation is not really that simple. Although failure demands correction, it does not automatically entail condemnation or punishment. On the one hand, the belief in *bechira chofshit*, free will, is a central pillar of our faith, and we clearly maintain that a person is held responsible for his choices. But sometimes, the choices that we make are not entirely free; they are partially "forced" upon us by circumstances. This is not an excuse for improper behavior, as every person is expected to overcome his circumstances and do what is right despite them. Nevertheless, those circumstances must still be taken into account in judging behavior.

Rav Soloveitchik addressed this topic through a discussion of a *gemara* in *Brachot* (31b-32a). In his presentation, he notes the particular circumstances of American Jewry in the 1950's, which were obviously quite different from the situation today. He thus speaks of the objective difficulty, the *nisayon*, faced by many Jews when told they would lose their jobs if they didn't show up for work on Shabbat; similarly, he mentions the difficulty in finding proper avenues of Jewish education for children in the days before day schools. Although these considerations and circumstances have changed, the Rav's point remains the same. We are now faced with different circumstances that make Torah observance difficult, but they must also be taken into account when rendering judgment.

The *gemara* discusses three biblical personalities who have one thing in common – they all complained to God when things weren't going well. They did not simply accept God's decree, but rather made their displeasure with *His* behavior known.

The *gemara* first discusses the nature and tone of Chana's prayer to God, when she implored Him to grant her a son:

"Now Chana was speaking upon (*al*) her heart."
Rabbi Elazar related in the name of Rabbi Yose ben Zimra: About matters that were [physically] upon her heart. She said before Him: "Master of the Universe! Of all that You created in a woman,

You did not create a single thing for naught. Eyes to
see, ears to hear, a nose to smell, a mouth to speak,
hands with which to do work, feet with which to
walk, and breasts with which to nurse. These breasts
that you have placed upon my heart, what are they
for? Are they not to nurse with? Grant me a child
that I may nurse with them!

According to this initial explanation of the verse, Chana's
prayer was not necessarily a complaint, but rather a *tefillah*
borne of bitterness. The *gemara* continues, however, to cite
an interpretation that clearly reads Chana's approach as one
of complaint:

...And Rabbi Elazar said: Chana flung words
upward to Heaven (*heticha devarim kelapei ma'alah*),
as it is stated, "And she prayed to (*al*) *Hashem*."
This teaches that she flung words upward toward
Heaven.

According to Rabbi Elazar, the fact that the verse uses
the unusual language of praying "*al Hashem*" instead of "*el
Hashem*" indicates that she not only vocalized her inner
bitterness; she also "flung words" towards God, complaining
about His injustice. Rashi explains that the phrase "*heticha
devarim*" presents an image of shooting arrows. Clearly, then,
Chana's tone was aggressive.

On the one hand, this approach to prayer seems to be
entirely inappropriate. Who is Chana to complain against
Ha-Kadosh Baruch Hu? On the other hand, Chana was
obviously no ordinary woman. Moreover, the result of her
prayer was that she indeed was blessed with a child. If her
tone was inappropriate or overwhelmingly negative, we

would not expect that she would be rewarded for her words!

The *gemara* then goes on to discuss another individual who "flung words upward toward Heaven" – Eliyahu Ha-Navi. As the great events at Har HaCarmel unfolded – after the prophets of Ba'al had attempted and failed to bring a fire down from their god to consume their sacrifice – it was Eliyahu's turn to demonstrate the power of God. He offered a brief prayer, "*Aneini Hashem aneini*," "Answer me, God, answer me," imploring God to respond to him and thereby demonstrate to the people that only God has power in this world. At that point, however, he added words to his prayer that require clarification:

> And Rabbi Elazar said: Eliyahu flung words upward to Heaven, as it is stated, "And You have turned their hearts backwards." Rabbi Shmuel bar Rabbi Yitzchak said: From where do we derive that the Holy One, blessed be He, concurred with Eliyahu? For it is written, "And the one whom I caused to be evil (*asher harei'oti*)."

Essentially, Eliyahu demands that God respond to his prayer because it is actually God's fault that all of this has happened; "*You* have turned their hearts backwards!" This is Your fault, Eliyahu tells God. And *Hashem* indeed concurs - *asher harei'oti* - it is I who has burdened man with the *yetzer ha'ra*.

Rashi explains that Eliyahu "blamed" God for giving man a *yetzer ha-ra*, the inclination to choose evil. It was God's fault that the people chose to worship *avoda zara*, because He granted them the evil inclination. This explanation is quite difficult to understand. After all, if God had not given us a *yetzer ha-ra*, then *bechira chofshit*, free will, would have been impossible, and if there were to be no free will and no moral conflict, there also could be no achievement in life. How, then, could Eliyahu complain that the Jews had been granted free will to choose idolatry?

Rav Soloveitchik suggests a different explanation. Eliyahu was complaining that God had placed *Am Yisrael* in such difficult circumstances that it is He who can be blamed, at least partially, for their failings. What do You expect?, Eliyahu said to God. The predominant culture in the country is that of Ba'al; the people of power, wealth, and influence are all associated with idolatry. In order to achieve success, one needed to join the Ba'al cult; otherwise, one would certainly be shunted aside without any voice or power. Indeed, many simple Jews who wanted to integrate into society most likely wondered: If God is so great, why isn't His presence felt? Why is His influence negligible? Eliyahu "flung words towards Heaven," declaring that the situation was of God's making, and it was therefore His responsibility to resolve it.

The Rav notes that the idea of circumstances influencing choice is also found in the episode of the "hardening of the heart" of Pharaoh, "*va-yachbed Hashem et lev Paro.*" Many commentaries question how God could have made it impossible for Pharaoh to make the right choice. If God negated Pharaoh's ability to choose freely, how could he then be punished for his obstinacy? If God forced him to take a certain path, how can he be held responsible? Ramban and Rambam explain that the hardening of Pharaoh's heart was actually a punishment for everything he did when he had the choice. When a person consistently chooses to do evil, God may take away his *bechira* and force him to remain in a world of evil. But this explanation is difficult; how can a person be prevented from doing *teshuva*? Even an instant before a person dies, he still has the opportunity to repent.

Ibn Ezra therefore argues that God never takes away anyone's *bechira* – but sometimes, God produces circumstances in life that make one's choices - indeed, one's very freedom and ability to choose - extremely difficult. God did not *prevent* Pharaoh from doing *teshuva*, but he made the circumstances so difficult for him to do so that he simply couldn't bring himself to repent. Pharaoh looked around him and saw that the entire Egyptian economy was dependent on Jewish slavery. How could he possibly let the Jews go? The Jew in the 1950's who chose to keep his shop open on Shabbat in order to make a living may have eventually changed his mind when his financial circumstances improved sufficiently so that it no longer remained necessary for him to work on Shabbat, and it was no longer as difficult a challenge to change. But a Jew who was still toiling in a sweatshop years after immigrating may have decided that he had no choice but to continue working each Shabbat. It was not as easy for him to do *teshuva*; his circumstances made it quite difficult. He still had the ability to do *teshuva*, but his situation made it much more complex.

This was Eliyahu's complaint against God. How can You expect *Am Yisrael* to go against the very society into which they seek to integrate, when they wish to adopt the culture of the society and accept the behavior of its leaders as normative? It takes extreme willpower to choose the path that is right in the face of great personal cost. The Jews who rejected Ba'al would not be accepted; they would not get the senior jobs or the best paying clients. You, God, produced the circumstances that made it extremely difficult for *Am Yisrael* to make the right choice.

Despite the apparent harshness of Eliyahu's accusation, the *gemara* tells us that God ultimately agreed with his assessment. In the Book of *Micha*, listed among those whom God will redeem are *"asher harei'oti,"* "those whom I caused to be evil." Rav Soloveitchik explains that God accepted Eliyahu's premise that when circumstances make *teshuva* difficult, those circumstances must be taken into account; it is as if God "caused" the person to be evil. The same actions of two different people may thus be judged very differently.

The third person who "flung words upward towards Heaven" was Moshe Rabbeinu:

> And Rabbi Elazar said: Moshe flung words upward towards Heaven, for it is stated, "And Moshe prayed to *Hashem*." Do not read this as "to *Hashem*" [*el* with an *aleph*], but rather as "against *Hashem* [*al* with an *ayin*]. For in the academy of Rabbi Eliezer ben Yaakov, they read *alephs* as *ayins* and *ayins* as *alephs*.

According to Rabbi Elazar, after the people complained in the incident of the *Mitonanim*, Moshe passed along their complaints to God. *Chazal* explain that the people were complaining about the three day forced march towards *Eretz Yisrael*, and Moshe conveyed their negative feelings to God Himself. Even though the *pasuk* uses the usual language of *"el"* to mean that Moshe prayed to God, Rabbi Elazar chooses to read the word as the more aggressive *"al,"* because the *pesukim* themselves do not reveal what Moshe said in his prayer. Since the Torah "covers up" what Moshe actually said, it must have been something critical.

The *gemara* goes on to offer another option:

> The scholars of the academy of Rabbi Yannai say: It can be derived from here: "and Di-Zahav." What is meant by "and Di-Zahav"? In the academy of Rabbi Yannai they say: Thus said Moshe before the Holy One, blessed be He: "Master of the Universe! Because of the silver and gold that You lavished (*she-hishpata*) upon Israel until they said, 'Enough!', that is what caused them to make the Golden Calf!

Among the places listed in the very beginning of *Sefer Devarim* is Di-Zahav, which, according to *Chazal*, is a hint to the *cheit ha-egel*. According to the scholars of the academy of Rabbi Yannai, Moshe here "flung words upward towards Heaven;" he accused God of being responsible for the sin of the people, by giving them too much gold and silver, to the point that they said, "*Dai*!" "Enough!"

Moshe was not simply complaining that God gave the people the materials necessary to construct the Golden Calf. He was rather suggesting that great wealth often leads to sin. Wealth corrupts, and especially wealth received as a "gift." For this reason, Moshe uses the word "*she-hishpata*," "that you lavished," which also means, "that you influenced." You blinded their eyes with wealth! What did You expect? We all know what often happens to poor people who suddenly win the lottery; their newfound wealth may utterly destroy them.

There is no excuse for the *cheit ha-egel*; indeed, *Chazal* say that every time the Jews sinned throughout the generations, some portion of the punishment for the *cheit ha-egel* is added on to the *onesh*. Nevertheless, Moshe argues, perhaps You are being too strict. Circumstances must be taken into account.

Ultimately, the *gemara* concludes, God agreed with Moshe's assessment:

> Rabbi Shmuel bar Nachmani said in the name of Rabbi Yonatan: From where do we derive that the Holy One, blessed be He, returned and concurred with Moshe? For it is stated, "And I lavished silver upon her, and gold, but they used it for Ba'al."

It is because I gave them so much gold and silver, God admits, that they went off to serve the Ba'al.

❧ CHALLENGE – NOT EXCUSE

Although the *gemara* presents three examples of people who "flung words upwards toward Heaven," who argued vehemently that circumstances must be taken into account, each of their arguments are essentially different from one another.

Chana argued that she had the right to be given the circumstances in which she could maximize her potential as a human being. In her view – despite her obvious intelligence and stature[26] – that meant that she be granted the ability to bear children. If You deny me the circumstances conducive to achieving that goal, she argued before God, I cannot stand before You as an *eved Hashem* in the full meaning of the word.

---

26 *Chazal* tell us that many of the *hilchot tefillah* are derived from Chana's prayer.

Eliyahu argued that *Am Yisrael* cannot be expected to be an *am kadosh* when all their circumstances were pulling them in the opposite direction. They were simply failing in a tug of war against a very formidable opponent, and their negative circumstances should be taken into account in judging them.

Moshe argued that it is sometimes specifically material success that creates circumstances that prevent the complete fashioning of an *oved Hashem*. *Am Yisrael* could not be expected to live up to God's expectations given the wealth that He had bestowed upon them.

The feeling that our circumstances have come in the way of our aspirations and dreams is not foreign to us. If only I had financial freedom, a man thinks, I could learn and study and achieve great things. Instead, I have to work hard for my money, and by the time I get home at night, there's no time to do all the things I've dreamed of doing. Looking back on his life, such a person feels that he has lost out because circumstances prevented him from doing what he really wanted to do with his life.

But the three examples noted by the *gemara* are not suggesting that we make excuses. The point is not that circumstances justify our failures; the point is that the flaws in our existence are challenges that must be overcome.

Chana did not accept her situation passively. She would not resignedly declare, "Now I have an excuse not to fulfill my destiny!" Instead, she went to the *Mishkan* and prayed, in an attempt to overcome her challenges. God gave her a child not because she surrendered to her circumstances, but rather because she tried to overcome them. Chana was not only critical; she accepted responsibility, recognizing that things can change if she were to take her destiny into her own hands.

The *Mitoninim* complained about a three-day march, which, in the larger scheme of things, does not seem that great a sacrifice for the sake of *Eretz Yisrael*. But Moshe pointed out that these were not seasoned veterans on the march, but rather slaves who didn't know what it means to be independent, proactive, and responsible. They had to continue on to *Eretz Yisrael* nevertheless, but Moshe's point was that the magnitude of their sin should be mitigated by considering their limited vision and shallow understanding of the context within which they were being commanded to obey God's will.

Similarly, the fire that God sent down from Heaven to consume Eliyahu's sacrifice did not solve the problem of the nation's idolatry; it simply got rid of their excuse. Now that the circumstances they were up against had changed, the people were expected to fall into line. When they didn't, punishment ultimately resulted in the form of the great destructions.

The pleas for understanding of circumstances, then, is essentially a request that God help us along a bit so that we can overcome those circumstances. This help may take the form of a victory in war that no one thought could be won or the small miracles that get us through the day – so that we can leave the excuses behind us.

❧ THREE VERSES

These ideas are reiterated in a statement made in the middle of this discussion in the *gemara* (32a):

Rabbi Chama the son or Rabbi Chanina said: Were it not for the following three verses, the legs of the enemies of Israel [euphemistically referring to *Am Yisrael*] would have collapsed. One verse is that which is written, "And the one I caused to be evil." (*Michah* 4:6) And one verse is that which is written, "Behold, as clay in the hand of the potter, so are you in My hand, O House of Israel." (*Yirmiyahu* 18:6) And one verse is that which is written, "And I will remove the heart of stone from your flesh and I will give you a heart of flesh." (*Yehezkel* 36:26)

Rashi, consistent with his approach throughout, explains all three verses as indicating that God is "responsible" for our failings because He gave us a *yetzer ha-ra*. You made us the way we are, we tell Him, so don't be surprised when we succumb to our evil inclination! Indeed, in the future, you will take away our *yetzer ha-ra* and replace it with a *yetzer tov*. It is the *yetzer ha-ra* that is the source of our failings; the design of the human being is flawed and we therefore cannot be held responsible.

As noted above, this approach is fraught with difficulty, as the rejection of the *yetzer ha-ra* entails rejection of the entire concept of *bechira chofshit*. Rav Solovetchik thus explains these three verses differently. As we saw, the verse "*asher harei'oti*" means that sometimes God places us in circumstances that make *teshuva* difficult. What is the message of the other two verses?

The second *pasuk*, "Behold, as clay in the hand of the potter, so are you in My hand, O House of Israel," "*Hinei ka-chomer be-yad ha-yotzer*," is quite familiar to us because it appears as a central motif in the *piyut* of Yom Kippur eve. In the original source (*Yirmiyahu* 18), God commands Yirmiyahu to go to a craftsman's shop, where he will deliver God's message. Yirmiyahu goes to the shop and sees the potter making pottery at his wheel. The potter's attempt to make a vessel failed, so he started from scratch, taking the unformed clay and refashioning it until he had achieved the final product that he desired. God explains to the prophet that this is a *mashal* for God's ability vis-à-vis *Am Yisrael*. I, too, He declares, can start all over again. I can threaten a nation that if they don't return to righteousness I will destroy them (as Yonah did), but if they do *teshuva*, I will "change my mind." On the other hand, if I had intended to do good to a people but they then change their ways, I will destroy them. Everything can be redone; it's up to you.

Interestingly, in the very next *perek*, Yirmiyahu is commanded to act out a similar *mashal*. He is told to buy a clay bottle, *bakbuk*, and take it to Gei Ben Hinnom, the valley in which the Jewish People committed the worst acts of *avoda zara*. There, he was to shatter the bottle in front of everyone, indicating that all would be destroyed.

Although they seem similar, there is actually a big difference between these *perakim*. In chapter 18, the vessel is still in formation; it can be fixed, reformed, and rebuilt. This is a message of hope, an encouragement that there is always a chance to start over again. The nations of the world, it seems, can literally change overnight. Thus, the people of Ninveh, the capital of the Assyrians, did *teshuva* in no time at all. But not long after, it was the Assyrians who destroyed the Kingdom of Israel and exiled the ten tribes. The nations can be formed and reformed, but their change has no staying power.

Chapter 19, in contrast, is talking specifically about *Am Yisrael*, who do not change nearly as easily. Forty eight *nevi'im* attempted to reform *Am Yisrael*, but nothing helped. We are the classic *am keshei oref*, the stiff-necked people who refuse to change. This trait is not entirely negative, however. Following the *cheit ha-egel*, Moshe entreats God to forgive the people for their sin, "*ki am keshei oref hu*" (*Shemot* 34:19). Rav Soloveitchik explains that it is specifically because the people are stiff-necked that they should be forgiven – because as hard as it is to reform them, once they accept something, they will never give it up.[27] It took two destructions to completely uproot *avoda zara* from the Jewish People, but once it was uprooted, they never returned to it. If you give them enough leeway, Moshe argued, they'll stick with you.

Klal Yisrael is not like the clay on the potter's wheel, but rather like the *bakbuk*, which can only see things correctly when it is threatened with utter destruction. Thus, it was during the time of Achashverosh and Haman that the people "*kimu mah she-kiblu kvar*," reaccepting the Torah that had been handed to them on a silver platter at Har Sinai. Indeed, we certainly don't have to look back that far in history to find points in time that shook us out of complacency. The message of such serious *shvira*, however, is not one of despair, but rather of an opportunity to overcome. These *shevirot* are not an excuse for bad behavior, but rather God's way of shaking us awake. The fact that our plans have not worked

---

27 Rav Soloveitchik interprets the word "*ki*" as "because." Many of the *mefarshim* attempt to grapple with this difficult verse by interpreting "*ki*" as "despite the fact" – "forgive the nation even though they are stiff necked."

out and that our hopes and dreams have not come to fruition does not entitle us to be *metiach devarim klapei shamaya*, to complain that God has not lived up to our expectations. Chana, Eliyahu, and Moshe did not teach us to simply bemoan our situation, but rather to make the necessary *cheshbon ha-nefesh* regarding how to take a bad situation and turn it around – and even build upon it.

The proof lies in the third *pasuk* quoted by the *gemara*. *Ha-Kadosh Baruch Hu* Himself promises that the day will come when He will intervene in history, when He will redeem His people. The *midrash* provides an interesting *mashal* in this regard. A poor maidservant went to draw water from a well, and her simple copper *kli* fell into the water. Saddened by the loss of her vessel, she began to cry. A maidservant of the king then arrived at the well, and she dropped her golden vessel into the well. Upon seeing this, the poor maidservant began to laugh. The king's maidservant asked why the girl was laughing at her suffering. The poor girl responded, "Now that yours fell in, they will surely come to fetch it – and then they'll bring mine back up too!" We are in *galut*, entrenched in suffering, and we cry. But if *Ha-Kadosh Baruch Hu* is with us, then we can be confident that when He picks Himself up, He will pick us up as well.

The reason God will ultimately redeem us is that He wishes to defend His name, to bring to an end the great *chillul* God caused by *galut*. Thus, the prophet Yechezkel tells us that God will redeem us because, "*ve-echmol al shem kodshi*," "I will have mercy on My holy name". Similarly, chapter 79 of *Tehillim*, which describes the great destruction caused by the nations in their attacks against us, begins "*Mizmor le-Asaf*," instead of the apparently more appropriate, *"Kina le-Asaf,"* because we are confident that God will save us to avoid a *chillul* of his Great Name; as we call out in *pasuk* 10, *"Lama yomru ha-goyim?"* We know for certain that God will one day remove our stumbling blocks and intervene in history. The promise of replacing our "stone hearts" with "hearts of flesh" is simply another way of indicating that the time will come when God will assist us in serving Him properly.

❧ THE *TESHUVA* OF YOM KIPPUR

Part of *teshuva* on Yom Kippur – perhaps the easiest part – is solving the simple equation of sin and repentance. If I committed a particular wrong, I should say the corresponding *Al Cheit*. The harder part of *teshuva* is when we look at all the circumstances of our lives and determine which ones are preventing us from achieving our goals on a personal and national level. We have no right to sit back and be complacent, to argue that we have been dealt a certain lot in life or certain limitations within which we must exist, and that there is nothing we can do about it. Chana, Eliyahu, and Moshe teach us to analyze the circumstances of our lives, determine how they have held us back – and then overcome them. If we truly believe that Israel should be built on principles of *chesed* and justice, then we must struggle to overcome any obstacles that stand in our way in achieving that goal. It is not acceptable to argue that our professional lives prevent us from enriching ourselves with Torah study and involvement in *chesed*. And if our wealth has introduced a foreign culture or negative influences into our home, then we must be wise enough and mature enough to neutralize those forces, for our sake and that of our children.

God gives us second chances to prove that we can overcome our circumstances. Our choice should not be to surrender to our circumstances, but rather to recognize that those circumstances are there to be overcome. On Yom Kippur, we should take stock of our personal and national circumstances so that we can take the opportunity to build ourselves and the world in accordance with God's wishes.

Blessings After Curses

─────────── ༄ ───────────

THE *GEMARA* (*MEGILLAH* 31B) CITES Rabbi Shimon Ben Elazar, who teaches that Ezra established that the *parshiot* of the *tochacha* are read at specific times during the year: the curses in *Torat Kohanim*, the *tochacha* of *Parshat Bechukotai*, should be read before Shavuot, while the curses of *Mishnah Torah*, the *tochacha* of *Parshat Ki Tavo*, should be read before Rosh Hashanah. This is in fact the custom to this day.

According to Abaye, the reason we read the *tochacha* before Rosh Hashana is "*kedei she-tichleh ha-shanah ve-kilelolteha*," so that the year should end with its curses behind us. Tosafot notes that according to this reasoning, *Parshat Ki Tavo* should be read on the Shabbat immediately preceding Rosh Hashana. In fact, however, the *parshiot* are broken up in such a way that *Parshat Nitzavim* is read on the last Shabbat of the year. One of the suggestions offered by Tosafot (which is brought as the *halacha* by the *Tur* and others) is that we want to create a gap between the curses in *Ki Tavo* and Rosh Hashana. We do not want to end the year with a reading of curses. We much prefer to read *Nitzavim*, which contains blessings and the *parsha* about *teshuva*, as well as mention of the *geulah*. *Parshat Nitzavim* is indeed uniquely suited for reading before the *Yamim Noraim*.

Upon considering the *tochacha* in *Parshat Ki Tavo*, we find that there is a significant difference between it and the *tochacha* in *Bechukotai*. The *tochacha* in *Bechukotai* ends with a blessing: "*Ve-zacharti et briti Yaakov ve-af et briti Yitzchak ve-af et briti Avraham ezkor, ve-ha-aretz ezkor,*" "And I will remember my covenant with Yaakov, and even my covenant with Yitzchak, and even my covenant with Avraham I will remember, and I will remember the land." This provides a form of "closure" to the curses, concluding the litany of destruction with the promise of future blessing. In *Ki Tavo*, by contrast, we find no such closure. In fact, the final *pasuk* in the *tochacha* there (29:68) speaks of *Hashem* bringing us back to Egypt in boats – with no happy ending in sight.

Upon closer examination, however, it appears that *Devarim* chapter 30, the central piece of *Nitzavim*, provides the "closure" missing from *Ki Tavo*, the first *pasuk* of the chapter being, "*Ve-hayah ki yavo alechah kol ha-devarim ha-eleh, ha-bracha ve-ha-kelalah,*" "And it will be when all of these things come to pass upon you, the blessing and the curse." This is a direct reference to the *brachot* and *klalot* in *Ki Tavo*.[28] *Parshat Nitzavim* essentially tells us what the proper

---

28 There are a number of instances in which the language of *pesukim* in

response is to the curses of *Parshat Ki Tavo* – introspection. Thus, the same verse continues, "*Ve-hashevota el levavecha*," "And you will contemplate it in your heart."

If this is so, why do these verses not appear in *Ki Tavo* immediately after the curses, in a similar presentation as *Bechukotai*? Ramban explains that the *tochacha* in *Bechukotai* refers to the *galut* following the destruction of the First Temple, which was short-lived – only 70 years long – whereas the *tochacha* of *Ki Tavo* refers to the *galut* following the destruction of the Second Temple, a *galut* which continues with no end in sight. Since the "closure" to the curses of *Ki Tavo* will not come immediately, it does not follow immediately in the Torah.

❧ *TESHUVA* AND *GEULA*

Parshat Nitzavim's description of the proper response to the curses of *galut* demands further clarification. Is "*ve-hashevota el levavecha*" – *teshuva* – a precondition that we must fulfill in order for the *geula* to arrive, or is it in fact one of the results of the *geula*? Is the process of repentance required before the *geula*, or will it be part of the process of

---

Nitzvaim parallel the language of the *tochacha* of *Ki Tavo*. For example, compare 30:3 – "And He will gather you from all of the nations to which He scattered you (*asher hefitzcha*)" – to 28:64 – "*Hashem* will scatter you (*ve-hefitzcha*) among all the nations." In another example, compare 30:5 – "And He will do good to you (*ve-hetivcha*) and multiply you (*ve-hirvecha*) more than your fathers" – with 28:63 – "To do good to you (*le-hetiv etchem*) and to multiply you (*ve-leharvot etchem*)." Similarly, 30:9 parallels 28:11, using the exact same wording referring to "the fruit of your womb and the fruit of your animals," with one *pasuk* using this phrase positively and the other negatively.

redemption when *Hashem* sees fit to bring the *geula*? This question is not one of semantics. It is in fact, subject to dispute among the *Rishonim*, and the answer will provide us with an important understanding of the process of *geula*, and of *teshuva* as an integral part of it.

Rambam (*Hilchot Teshuva* 7:5) cites our *pasuk*, "*ve-hashevota el levavecha*," as a source for the idea that the Torah promises that there will be a *teshuva* process, just as there will be a *geula*. Rambam clearly understands the verse as indicating that *teshuva* is one of the results – not one of the conditions – of the *geula* process.

The opinion of Ramban, however, is more ambiguous. Later in *Nitzavim*, the Torah tells us (30:11), "This *mitzva* which I have commanded you today is not too difficult for you, nor is it far off." Ramban understands this *pasuk* as referring to the *mitzva* of *teshuva*, as the previous ten *pesukim* deal with the subject of repentance. He is therefore of the opinion that there is a *mitzvat asei*, an obligation, to do *teshuva*. Ramban further writes that the *geula* is dependant upon us fulfilling the *mitzva* of *teshuva*, but at the same time, *Hashem* promises us that such *teshuva* will occur. Ramban acknowledges that this explanation is ambiguous, but this is because the Torah itself is ambiguous, using language that he calls "*safa beinonit*," language that can be interpreted both as a command and a prediction.[29]

---

29 The most famous example of this type of language is in the *parsha* dealing with the appointment of a king (*Devarim* 17:15): "When you come to the land, *ve-amarta* [you **should** say/you **will** say], 'Let me appoint a king upon myself.'" Shmuel HaNavi was aghast at the people's request for a king. Why would he have reacted this way if appointing a king is a *mitzva* whose time had come? Ramban explains that the word "*ve-amarta*" is *lashon beinoni*,

❧ DIFFERENT TYPES OF *TESHUVA*

Chapter 30 in *Parshat Nitzavim* describes the complex process of *teshuva* in detail, illustrating that the "dialogue" of *teshuva* between the people and *Hashem* has various stages. Rav Aharon Lichtenstein notes that there are also different forms of *teshuva*. The *teshuva* that we are familiar with, the intense process undergone before Yom Kippur, is primarily an individual's *teshuva* for his personal failures, what Rav Lichtenstein terms the "*teshuva* of the norm." In reality, this *teshuva* is tied not to Yom Kippur, but to the occurrence of sin; it should be performed immediately upon recognition that one has erred. As Rambam writes in *Hilchot Teshuva*, the connection between Yom Kippur and this form of *teshuva* is to be found in the fact that Yom Kippur is simply an opportune time to do *teshuva* because *Hashem* is to be found closer to us during this time period.

There is another type of *teshuva* as well, which Rav Lichtenstein calls the "*teshuva* of crisis." This type of *teshuva* is not a response to an individual sin. Instead, a crisis serves as a catalyst for renewing one's relationship with *Hashem*, providing solace from the crisis. This can result when a person feels that he has distanced himself from *Hashem* and that he needs to renew his relationship with *Hashem*.

We find a parallel distinction in the views of Rambam and Ramban regarding the nature of the *mitzva* of prayer. Rambam maintains that there is a positive commandment to pray to *Hashem* once a day, while Ramban maintains that

---

both a *mitzva* and a prediction.

there is a positive commandment to pray to *Hashem* only when a person is "*be-tzarah*" or "*be-metzukah*," in sorrow or distress. The *tefillah* that Ramban describes, prayer out of crisis, gives rise to the halachic obligation of *teshuva*. Thus, the resolution of crises is dependent on doing *teshuva*.[30]

Whereas this crisis may be internal, it is often an external event that forces a person or a nation to turn to *Hashem*. The opening *pasuk* in chapter 30 describes such an external crisis, the crisis of living in *galut* among the nations. Such external circumstances drive us to *teshuva*, with the following *pesukim* describing the subsequent dialogue between *Hashem* and the nation. In this dialogue, we see evidence of that famous saying of *Chazal*, in which *Hashem* declares, "Open for me an opening the size of the eye of an needle, and I will open an opening in the heavens for you in which chariots can pass through!" (*Midrash Rabbah Shir HaShirim* 5:3) The *pesukim* describe how our initial *teshuva* is rewarded with multiple blessings, including a return to *Eretz Yisrael*.

In *pasuk* 6, a new part of the process is described: "*U-mal Hashem Elokecha et levavcha.*" *Hashem* will remove the blockages from our hearts that *Chazal* tell us prevent our hearts from finding the true expression of our love for *Hashem*. Some commentators explain that the return to *Eretz Yisrael* will cause a removal of this blockage; we will return to our natural relationship with *Hashem* via our return to *Eretz Yisrael*.

In *pasuk* 8, however, something strange happens, as we

---

30 Rambam hints to this in *Hilchot Ta'anit* as well, where he writes that the *mitzva* to blow the *shofar* on a fast day is a form of *tefillah*, of turning to *Hashem* during a time of crisis.

are told once again what we already read in *pesukim* 1 and 2 – that we will return and keep all of the *mitzvot*. What is the reason for this repetition?

Commentators from around the time of the Spanish Inquisition, such as the Abarbanel and the Ba'al Ha-Akedah, write that *pasuk* 8 refers to the Marranos. At the height of their persecution, the Marranos had returned in their hearts; they knew the Torah, but they couldn't observe it. In *pasuk* 1, the *teshuva* process includes only "*ve-shamata*," "and you shall listen;" *pasuk* 8 adds the word, "*ve-asita*," "and you shall keep," teaching that these Jews will also complete the *teshuva* process and will also be redeemed.[31]

Or Ha-Chayim suggests that these *pesukim* describe the *geula* as a three-step process. First, "*ve-shemata be-kolo*" (30:2), a return to learning Torah. At that point, the "*milat ha-lev*" (30:6) will take place, and the nation will observe all of the negative commandments. Finally, "*ve-asita*" (30:8) – the nation will keep the positive *mitzvot* as well.

Rav Lichtenstein offers an alternate solution, describing a form of *teshuva* that is very relevant today – the *teshuva* of *shichecha*, repentance of forgetfulness. The Halacha repeatedly refers to the concept of "*hesech ha-da'at*," literally "removal of one's mind" from what one is doing. For example, while one is wearing *tefillin*, he may not remove his attention from them even momentarily; since they are objects of holiness, one must be continuously conscious of them.[32] Similarly, if a

---

31 Abarbanel wrote three seforim on the process of *geula*, in which he builds on these *pesukim*. He viewed the Spanish Inquisition as being the ultimate fulfilment of the curses, to the point that he felt that the *geula* was imminent.

32 The *gemara* notes that the *Kohen Gadol* was required to be consciously aware

Kohen has *hesech ha-da'at* from *terumah* in his possession, he may no longer eat it.

Rav Lichtenstein argues that going about your day with *hesech ha-da'at* of *Hashem* creates a flaw (figuratively speaking) in the presence of *Hashem*. This is a form of *chilul Hashem* and it demands *teshuva*. Rav Lichtenstein notes that there are two types of *"Al Cheit"*s that we say on Yom Kippur – those that relate to a particular sin and those that relate to the creation of conditions that lead to sin. An example of this second type is *"Al cheit she-chatanu lefanecha beli da'at,"* which is typically translated as referring to transgressions arising out of lack of knowledge. Rav Lichtenstein explains that we can also say that this very lack of knowledge is itself a sin. The fact that we do not continually focus on *Hashem* as being the central element in our lives is in itself sinful.

The sin of *hesech ha-da'at*, Rav Lichtenstein explains, occurs when a person reaches his level of comfort in observance and feels no need to improve any further; his ambition comes to a halt. It is the sin of complacency, of creating a state in which *Hashem* is marginalized in our lives.

Pesukim 1 and 2 describe *teshuva* out of crisis, after which we are brought back to *Eretz Yisrael, Hashem* takes revenge on our enemies, and our hearts are open to express our love of *Hashem* – an ideal situation. Unfortunately, ideal situations have been historically bad for us; once the crisis or danger has passed, we slip back into our old ways. After receiving all the good from *Hashem*, we promptly forget him, and we have

---

of the *tzitz* that he wore on his head, and *Hashem*'s name was ingraved on it only once. How much more so must one be aware of the *tefillin*, in which *Hashem*'s name appears twenty-one times!

to do *teshuva* again. This is the *teshuva* described in *pasuk* 8.

In this second *teshuva*, however, the impetus is not crisis, but rather self-motivation. It results from recognizing our *hesech ha-da'at*, that we have forgotten to make *Hashem* the central focus of our lives. Once this *teshuva* has been achieved, *pasuk* 9 tells us, *Hashem* will be happy with us, just as He was happy with our *Avot*.

This process is also illustrated in chapter 10 of Rambam's *Hilchot Teshuva*. After elucidating all the details of *teshuva*, the Rambam returns to discuss the concept of *avahat Hashem*, being "love-sick" for Hashem. The first stage of *teshuva* entails simply returning to observance, but keeping Torah and *mitzvot* without passion is *hesech ha-da'at*. To reach the final *geula* of *Parshat Nitzavim*, we need to overcome this *hesech ha-da'at* and re-attain this passion.

Seeing the
World Differently

─────────── ✤ ───────────

The *gemara* in *Brachot* (16b-17a) cites a number of *tefillot* that the *Amora'im* composed. For example, the *tefillah* that we recite as part of *Birchat Ha-Chodesh* – "*She-techadesh aleinu et ha-chodesh ha-zeh le-tovah u-livracha*" – was personally composed by Rav, and he recited it every day at the end of his *Shemoneh Esrei*. Another *Amora* composed the *tefillah*, "*Elokai neshama she-natata bi tehora hi*," which we have incorporated into our daily *tefillot*. Rav Soloveitchik explained that we can achieve a better understanding of each of these special *tefillot* by analyzing the personality of its author. Why did that particular person write this particular prayer?

One of these *tefillot* was penned by Rav Sheshet, who

would recite it after he finished his *davening* on fast days:

> Master of the World – it is known to You that
> at the time that the *Beit Ha-Mikdash* stood, if a
> person sinned, he would offer a sacrifice. And he
> would offer only its fat and blood, and it would
> atone for him. And now [that there is no longer a
> *Beit Ha-Mikdash*], I have fasted and my own fat and
> blood have diminished. May it be Your will that
> my diminished fat and blood should be considered
> before You as though I have sacrificed upon the
> altar, and You should be appeased by me.

Unlike a *korban olah*, which was entirely burnt upon
the *mizbei'ach*, a *korban chatat* only entailed the burning of
the fat and blood, but even so, this was sufficient to provide
atonement for the one offering the *korban*. In the absence
of the *Beit Ha-Mikdash*, Rav Sheshet prays, our fasts should
serve as a replacement for the *korban chatat*, as they deplete
our fat and blood reserves. Indeed, this *tefillah* has been
incorporated into the *Tefillat Zakah* recited before *Kol Nidrei*,
in which we ask that the hunger that we experience on Yom
Kippur should be considered the equivalent of a *korban*.

~ RAV SHESHET "SEES" THE KING

Why is this *tefillah* particular to Rav Sheshet? What was
it about Rav Sheshet's personality that made this particular
prayer appropriate for him? Rav Soloveitchik cited another
gemara in *Brachot* (58a) that relates that Rav Sheshet was a
"*sagi nahor*" – he was blind. Immediately after discussing the
appropriate blessing to recite upon seeing a human king, the

gemara tells the following story:

> The entire populace went out to the street to greet the king, and Rav Sheshet went with them. He encountered a *Tzeduki* (Saduccee). He said to him: When you go down to the river to bring up water, you take a complete pitcher with you. But a broken pot – where are you taking it?

The *Tzedukim* were heretics who did not believe in *Torah She-Ba'al Peh*, and the conflict between them and the *Perushim* began during the time of the *Beit Ha-Mikdash* and was still apparent at the time of the *gemara*. This particular *Tzeduki* was apparently quite rude, boldly implying that there was no point in Rav Sheshet going out to greet the king along with the rest of the town. After all, everyone else was going to see the king, and Rav Sheshet couldn't see.

> He said to him: Come and I will show you that I know matters better than you. The first battalion passed by. Upon hearing the noise, the *Tzeduki* said to him: The king is coming. Rav Sheshet said to him: The king is not coming. The second battalion passed by. Upon hearing the noise, the *Tzeduki* said to him: Now the king is coming. Rav Sheshet said to him: The king is not coming.

When the *Tzeduki* heard the cheering of the crowds, he assumed that the king was coming, but the arrival of the next battalion of soldiers proved him wrong twice. Indeed, when the third battalion marched by, the *Tzeduki* kept quiet – he didn't want to take the chance that he would be wrong again!

> A third battalion passed by, and then there was silence. Rav Sheshet said to him: The king is certainly

coming now. The *Tzeduki* said to him: How do you know this? He said to him: The kingdom of this world is similar to the Kingdom of Heaven (*malchuta de-ara ke-ein malchuta de-rakia*). As it says, "Go out and stand on the mountain before *Hashem*. And behold, *Hashem* was passing, and a great and powerful wind that breaks mountains and shatters boulders passed before *Hashem* – but *Hashem* was not in the wind. And after the wind, an earthquake – but *Hashem* was not in the earthquake. And after the earthquake a fire – but *Hashem* was not in the fire. And after the fire, the sound of soft silence (*kol demama daka*)... (*Melachim I* 19:11-12)"

When the king came, Rav Sheshet recited the *bracha*. The *Tzeduki* said to him: Can someone who does not see the king recite the *bracha*? And what became of that *Tzeduki*? Some say that his colleagues [the *Tzedukim*] gouged his eyes out. And some say that Rav Sheshet glanced at him and he turned into a heap of bones.

The *mefarshim* and *poskim* bring proof from this *gemara* that even a blind person should make this *beracha*. In order to qualify to recite this blessing, one need not see the king with his physical eyes, but rather be aware of his presence. Along those lines, Rav Sheshet explained to the *Tzeduki* that even a blind man can tell when the king is coming, because he is preceded by the sound of silence – just as *Hashem*'s presence is manifest in the *kol demama daka*.[33]

---

33 Indeed, this image is portrayed in *U-Netaneh Tokef*. While the process of

This entire episode leaves us with a question, of course. Why was Rav Sheshet so convinced that "the kingdom of this world is like the Kingdom of Heaven"? Why was he so sure that this human king would follow the script of *Melachim Alef*? How is it that the blind Rav Sheshet knew better than the brazen *Tzeduki* that the king was indeed coming?

Upon closer analysis, it is clear that this was the first time anyone in Rav Sheshet's town – including Rav Sheshet and the *Tzeduki* – had ever witnessed a regal procession. If they had any experience in such matters, no one would have had to guess when the king was coming; it would have been apparent to all that three battalions would pass first.

Moreover, it seems apparent that the people made a great noise, cheering and yelling, when they saw all the pomp and circumstance of the soldiers, because they assumed that this indicated that the king was right behind, and they assumed that this was the appropriate way to greet him. For whatever reason, we make some noise – even the sound of polite handclapping – to express our joy at being in the presence of greatness. The *Tzeduki* – a man representing a belief system that relies only on the written word, on firsthand experience, and upon what can be seen, while denying the validity of anything else – falls for the same trap. When the *Tzeduki* sees the soldiers, he concludes that the king must be coming, and he claps along with everyone else.

But Rav Sheshet knew something that the *Tzeduki* did not. The blind Rav Sheshet realized that noise means

---

judgment begins with "*U-ba-shofar gadol yitaka*," it is only after "*Ve-kol demama daka yishama*" that the *malachim* go into a frenzy and declare, "*Hinei yom ha-din!*"

nothing. Before the king actually did arrive, the entire crowd – made up of people who had never seen the king before – was absolutely silent. They felt that the king was coming; there was something intangible in the air. Something told them to stop all the noise and remain silent out of awe, even though they couldn't define it. Rav Sheshet felt it too, but he knew that that mysterious silence is the sign of the presence of greatness – the *kol demama daka*. He felt the same thing everyone else in the crowd felt, but he could identify the feeling because he knew that "the kingdom of this world is like the Kingdom of Heaven." Indeed, that is the very reason that *Chazal* instituted the wording for the blessing upon seeing a king – "*Baruch she-chilek mi-kvodo le-basar va-dam*," "Blessed is the One who gave over from His honor to flesh and blood." Something about the presence of a human king approximates the presence of *Ha-Kadosh Baruch Hu* .

The *Tzeduki*, in contrast, refused to give in to the intangible feeling, the sense of awe, allowing himself to be guided only by what he sees, what he knows, what is written. Everyone else seems to know that the king is coming, but the *Tzeduki* must still ask how Rav Sheshet is so sure. If his vision couldn't prove it, the *Tzeduki* simply couldn't believe it.

It is for this very reason, Maharsha explains, that the *Tzeduki* harassed Rav Sheshet from the very beginning of the story, comparing him to a broken vessel. In his view, there was no point in coming to "see" the king when you cannot actually see him, and one certainly cannot recite the blessing under such circumstances. In his view, only what one can see with his own eyes can be verified as real. Rav Sheshet, in contrast, relied on his *shemia*, his hearing. When he "heard" the *kol demama daka* – essentially, the absence of sound – he realized that it was significant.

❧ THE *MERAGLIM* AND *TZITZIT*

Rav Soloveitchik noted that because Rav Sheshet was blind, he could make a point that no one else could – that seeing is not only a function of the physical sense of sight, of what one's eyes actually see. Sight entails spiritual perception as well, sensing the meaning and significance of something.[34]

This meaning of sight is conveyed in the juxtaposition of the *parshiot* of the *Meraglim* and the *mitzva* of *tzitzit*. The spies relied on their physical vision alone, and it led them astray; they returned with a report of everything that they "saw" – the giants and the fortresses. But they failed to interpret what they had seen properly. While their report was entirely accurate on the physical plane, they forgot to contemplate what they had witnessed; they failed to truly "see" its significance because they neglected to recall that *Hashem* could overcome all of the obstacles.

In contrast, in the *parsha* of *tzitzit*, the Torah teaches us how to properly see – "*U-re'item oto u-zechartem et kol mitzvot Hashem.*" For every four or eight strands of *tzitzit*, there is one strand of *techelet* to remind us that not everything is so simple. While things may appear to be "white" – the color of simplicity and clarity – there is also "blue" – the color that reminds us of the *kisei ha-kavod*. When we look at the blue

---

34 This sense of sight is often conveyed by the word "*le-histakel*," rather than, "*lir'ot*." Thus, when *Chazal* say, "*Al tistakel be-kankan*," they are not telling us not to look at the vessel, but rather not to only consider it.

strand of *techelet*, we realize that the perceived world before us is only a small fraction of the larger reality. There's a lot going on out there that we don't see with our eyes, but it is no less real for that. The *techelet* reminds us that we cannot allow ourselves to be complacent, settling for what we see with our eyes without making the effort to think more deeply about reality. The *techelet* of the *tzitzit* is the *tikun* of the sin of the *Meraglim*, who sinned because they misunderstood how to properly use their sight.

In order to truly see, one cannot be satisfied with what his eyes tell him, as was the *Tzeduki*. Instead, one must view the world the way that Rav Sheshet did – associating what one sees with what he knows, analyzing and thinking deeply in order to reach true conclusions.

Indeed, the *parsha* of *tzitzit* itself warns about the dangers of following after one's eyes, as that type of sight can be misleading – "*Ve-lo taturu acharei levavchem ve-acharei eineichem*." Instead, we are commanded to see the *ptil techelet*, to remind ourselves of the deeper reality that we exist in.

❧ *CHELEV* AND *DAM*

How does this story about Rav Sheshet's "sight" inform our understanding of his *tefillah* on fast days?

Rav Soloveitchik explained the significance of Rav Sheshet's choice of words in his prayer. Rav Sheshet noted that the fast depletes one's *chelev* and *dam*, his fat and blood, and this should serve in the stead of the fat and blood of the *korban chatat*. According to the *sifrei mussar*, and even dating back to Rambam in *Moreh Nevuchim*, excess fat reflects over-indulgence, falling prey to non-essentials. Blood, in contrast, is essential. There can be no life without it. Sometimes, sin comes from *chelev*, one's need for the indulgences that he is used to. Even though non-kosher food is obviously not essential to one's survival, he feels that he simply must have it because, in his own mind, he "can't live without it." On the other hand, some sins are the result of *dam*, not the need to indulge but rather due to the need to maintain the barest necessities of life. Someone whose financial situation deteriorates may cut corners in his business, doing things he never would have dreamed of doing in the past, because he finds himself in a situation in which he sees no other option.

Chelev and *dam* are the symbols of two types of *cheit* that blind us, that make it impossible for us to see things as they really are. If we were to see that indulging is just that – unnecessary – we would not sin. If we were able to see that the necessities of life may push us into the corner of *cheit*, where we don't really want to be, we wouldn't just see the red ink at the bottom of our monthly statement. At the time of the *Beit Ha-Mikdash*, when a person offered a *korban chatat*, he burnt both the *chelev* and the *dam* – symbolically teaching the sinner that in order to achieve forgiveness, he must break the pattern of *cheit*, the basis of which is in the *chelev* and the *dam*. By sacrificing the *chelev* and the *dam*, we set before ourselves the goal of breaking down these obstructions to our clearer vision.

In his *tefillah*, Rav Sheshet articulated that now that we have no *korban chatat*, we sacrifice the *chelev* and *dam* through our fasts, thereby similarly breaking the pattern of *cheit*. On fast days, there is no indulgence in chocolate cake and whipped cream – no *chelev*. We do not even partake in the barest necessities, like bread and water – there is no *dam*. Through our act of *tzom* we prove that indulgence and even necessity are external to us, and once we separate from them, we can see more clearly.

This *tefillah* was particularly suited to Rav Sheshet, who was able to distinguish between physical vision, which he lacked, and true vision. Rav Sheshet taught that what we should really be seeing is that indulgences and necessities are not part of us, that we can become independent from them. The blind Rav Sheshet preached that in order to conquer *cheit*, one must look at life differently. In his view, *teshuvah* does not only entail quantitative change, acceptance of more Torah learning and *kiyum ha-mitzvot*, as important as that is. Rav Sheshet demands a paradigm shift, a qualitative change in one's *avodat Hashem*.

I had a rebbe in High School who presented me with one such paradigm shift and changed the way I look at the world. He noted that most committed Jews, if asked, would define themselves as essentially no different from non-Jews on a human level. We are different because we have an *additional* obligation to fulfill Torah and *mitzvot*. My rebbe said that this is a big mistake. In reality, God created a world whose entire purpose is the fulfillment of the Torah and *mitzvot*. He wanted there to be a *mitzva* of *tefillin*, and in order for it to be fulfilled, He needed to create people with arms. You are not first a person, and in addition to being a person like any other, you are obligated as a Jew, to don *tefillin*; first, there is the will of God, who wishes that there be a mitzvah of *tefillin*, and it is in order for that to be fulfilled that we exist, our arms exist, and so forth. You exist *because* there is a *mitzva* of *tefillin* – in order to fulfill the *ratzon Elokim*. This is what *Chazal* meant when they said (*Kedushin* 82a), "*ani nivreiti le-shamesh koni*" – " I was created only to serve my Master."

This is what Rav Sheshet meant. With our physical eyes, we look around us and see that the world is full of all kinds of people going about their business, and we exist just like them. They have their lives, and I have mine; they have their countries, and I have mine. In addition, I was lucky – I was at Har Sinai and I received the Torah. When we look at the world with Rav Sheshet's glasses, however, we see a world that was created so that the will of God would be fulfilled. I exist because I have a role to play in fulfilling the *ratzon Elokim*.

The *Aseret Yemei Teshuva* is a time to add to our *kiyum ha-Torah* and *mitzvot* and to desist from deviations we have been guilty of in the past – but it is not only that. It is a time to sacrifice our *chelev* and *dam*, to remove the blinders that make us feel that living our lives is a separate idea from living Torah, the purpose of our existence. Once we achieve this type of sight, we become vehicles for the fulfillment of *Hashem*'s will on this earth. When we look at life this way, the difficulties in the choices that we sometimes have to make seem to melt away. If we view ourselves as vehicles for the fulfillment of *Hashem*'s will, then everything is viewed through that prism, and then everything suddenly becomes clear.[35] The *kol demama daka* that people sense intuitively as

---

35 This is perhaps the reason that *Shulchan Aruch* begins the very first *halacha*

predicting the coming of the *Shechinah* is that inner feeling that we experience by virtue of the very fact that we look at life in a different way.

Rav Soloveitchik noted that this is the objective of every *yom tzom*, and this lesson seems especially relevant to Yom Kippur. When we separate ourselves somewhat from the normal amenities of physical life, we can see more clearly that life as *shomrei Torah u-mitzvot* is not about living plus Torah, but rather about living Torah.

❧ A LESSON APPLICABLE TO ALL

The fact that the Torah commands us "*u-re'item oto u-zechartem et kol mitzvot Hashem*" indicates that we are all capable of achieving this level of adapting our vision so that we can see the truth. If only someone of the stature of Rav Sheshet could look at life from the right perspective, then the Torah would not have commanded such a *mitzva* to one and all. Rav Sheshet was critical of the *Tzeduki* because in Rav Sheshet's opinion, the *Tzeduki* should have been able to do exactly what Rav Sheshet did. Indeed, the *Tzeduki* was punished because he should have been able to accomplish what Rav Sheshet had; instead, he was unwilling to open his heart to feelings beyond what his physical eyes could see, and he suffered the consequences.

---

with a guide to practical observance of the *mitzvot* – that one should always say to himself, "*Shiviti Hashem le-negdi tamid.*" If we train ourselves to realize that our existence is a constant relationship between us and *Ha-Kadosh Baruch Hu*, then everything else becomes self-understood; nothing is a struggle anymore.

As we get older, life teaches us that what we once thought was important, what we once thought were insurmountable barriers to advancement in *kiyum ha-Torah*, are suddenly not so important anymore. They've lost their sheen. What's left are those potent moments of *kol demama daka*. For many of us, myself included, one such moment is when the *aron ha-kodesh* is opened immediately before *Kol Nidrei* and the *sifrei Torah* are taken out. The *chazan* and the elders of the community are standing around the *bima*, and everyone is standing at attention in their freshly ironed *kittels*. That procession of *sifrei Torah* from the *aron* to the *bima* is very different from the one on *Simchat Torah*. At the beginning of *Kol Nidrei*, there is a feeling of *kol demama daka*; we sense the presence of the *Shechinah* amongst us, and everyone is intuitively quiet. At that moment, there is an intangible feeling that the *ruach* has passed and the *ra'ash* has passed and the *aish* has passed, and now there is only the sound of silence. At that moment, as we are about to begin our fast, and sacrifice our *chelev* and *dam*, as we are about to ask *Hashem* for his forgiveness and the blessing of a *shana tova* – at that moment, we should take advantage of the overpowering feeling of identity with the *Shechinah*. We should somehow capture that moment and take it with us, so that it remains in our hearts even after the doors of the *aron kodesh* are closed.

The *Ikveta* De-Mashicha

───── ✥ ─────

THE *MISHNAYOT* AT THE end of *Sotah* (48a-49a)
trace the historical process of the *churban*, noting that as an
increasing number of the traditional foundational institutions
of *Klal Yisrael* ceased to exist, the very fabric of society was
affected:

> When the Sanhedrin was dissolved, there was
> no longer song in the drinking houses... When
> the early prophets died, the *Urim Ve-Tumim* was
> no longer used... From the day that the *Beit Ha-
> Mikdash* was destroyed, there is no day that does
> not contain some measure of curse, and the dew has
> not fallen for blessing, and the taste of the fruit has
> been taken away...

The process of *galut* destroys the very core of Jewish society,
disrupting it entirely and leading to its ultimate collapse.

But that very process is actually the beginning of another process – the process of *geulah*. It is the complete disintegration of Jewish life that is actually the harbinger of redemption. The *mishnah* provides us with a particular roadmap, a description of what life will be like in the "*Ikveta de'Mashicha*," the time of the "footsteps of *Mashiach*" (*Sotah* 49b).

First, "*chutzpa yasgeh*" – the phenomenon of *chutzpa* will simply explode and take hold of everyone. Furthermore, there will be economic signs that the *geulah* is upon us. "*Yoker ya'amir*" – prices will skyrocket; "*Ha-gefen titein piryah ve-ha-yayin be-yoker*" – the vines will give forth grapes, but wine will still be expensive. Despite the ample supply, prices will remain high. Rav Kehati explains that this is because the wine will be drunk faster than it can be produced; everyone will be drunkards!

The *mishnah* goes on to describe that "*ha-malkchut tehefoch le-minut*" – the rulers will be heretics – "*ve-ein tochacha*" – there will be no one to rebuke them. No one will be able to convince the rulers to change their improper ways, apparently because everyone in a position of influence will either himself be a party to this type of behavior or will be too scared to say anything. "*Beit va'ad yihiyeh li-znut*" – the institutions that had been the centers of Torah learning will instead be used for the opposite type of activities.

Interestingly, one of the signs that the *geulah* is soon to arrive is "*ha-Galil yecherav*," the Galil will be destroyed. Before the *churban*, the Galil constituted most of *Eretz Yisrael*. The fact that the *mishnah* says that this region will be destroyed before the redemption implies that before that stage, the Galil will be rebuilt! Before the *ikvot de-mashicha*, there will be a vibrant Jewish presence in the Galil. Similarly, "*ve-ha-Gavlan yishom.*" Some *meforshim* explain that this is a reference to the Golan (a composite of "*Golan ba-Bashan*"). Whereas before the Golan had been full of people, it will now be laid waste, *shomem*.

The *mishnah* continues: "*Ve-anshei ha-gevul yesovevu mei-ir la-ir ve-lo yechunanu*" – the people living on the borders, outside the main centers of Jewish habitation, will move from city to city and no one will show them grace. Apparently, they will be forced to travel in search of help in maintaining the viability of their strategic home towns. But they will have to continue to wander, as no one will provide them with the necessary assistance.

Moreover, "*chochmot sofrim tisrach*" – people will no longer respect the wisdom of the scholars. "*Yirei cheit yimasu*" – God fearing people will be despised. Those who follow in *Hashem*'s ways will meet only with contempt on the part of the people. "*Ha-emet tehei ne'ederet*" – truth will be "missing," as it will no longer be a value worth preserving. "*Ne'arim penei zekeinim yalbinu*" – the youth will have no respect for the older generation, embarrassing and humiliating them. "*U-zekeinim ya'amdu mipnei ketanim*" – out of fear, the older people will stand for the younger generation. Instead of the young honoring the old, the old will have to show respect for the young. This lack of respect will even persist within the family unit: "*Ben minabel av, bat kama be-imah, kala be-chamota*" – sons will rise up against their fathers, daughters against their mothers, and daughters-in-law against their mothers-in-law. "*Oyvey ish anshei beito*" – the members of one's household will be his enemies. "*Pnei ha-dor ke-pnei ha-kelev*" – no one in that generation will show proper respect.

This is indeed a chilling description of the degree to which society can degenerate – to the point at which all of our most basic values are turned upside down. The *mishnah* seems to realize how very disheartening this description is, concluding, "*Ve-al mi yesh lanu le-hisha'en? Al Avinu she-ba-shamayim*." When the time comes that the concept of respect will be entirely lost, who will we be able to rely upon? Only on our Father in Heaven. When society has hit rock-bottom, when the world is topsy turvy, *Ha-Kadosh Baruch Hu* will set things straight by bringing the *geulah*.

There is another possible reading of this line, however. Instead of interpreting this phrase as providing the solution to all of the preceding troubles, it may be adding to the list of signs of the *ikveta de-Meshicha*. "*Al mi yesh lanu le-hisha'en? Al Avinu she-ba-shamayim*" is also a *siman* that the *geulah* is coming. In a normal, healthy society, we would take steps to resolve our problems; we would not simply turn to God to provide miraculous salvation. Although we would obviously ask for Divine assistance, we would take the necessary steps to turn things around, to revamp our educational system, to shake our young people out of their disrespect. But in the *ikvata de-Mashicha*, in the face of the degeneration of society and family, the only response will be to raise our hands to Heaven in helplessness.

In his *Orot Ha-Teshuva*, Rav Kook stresses that without relating to the specific characteristics of one's generation, it is impossible to develop appropriate and effective solutions to guide *Klal Yisrael* towards *teshuva*. Every age, Rav Kook explains, is a function of its unique characteristics, its own *techunot*.

Many generations have determined, based on the *mishnah* we have studied, that they lived at the time of the *ikveta de-Mashicha*, and it obviously turned out that they were wrong. Nevertheless, this *mishnah* is helpful in putting our own times in perspective and enlightening us towards signs of the historical process that is transpiring before our eyes. In this way, our *mishnah* can guide us to the proper path of *teshuva* for our generation.[36]

❧ CHACHAM ADIF MI-NAVI

In an essay entitled, "*Chacham Adif Mi-Navi*," Rav Kook analyzes the significant historical process that has taken place in *Klal Yisrael* from the time of *nevuah* to our very day. He describes a division of labor between the *Nevi'im* and the *Chachamim*, distinguishing between two types of perspective.

---

36 One might argue that this enterprise goes against the concept of *temimut*, the imperative to "go innocently" with *Hashem*. On the *pasuk*, "*tamim tihiyeh im Hashem Elokecha*," Ramban writes that we should not analyze every individual occurrence that happens in order to see what the future holds. *Temimut* means that one must accept what *Ha-Kadosh Baruch Hu* does as being subject to His wisdom, not our own. One must accept the fact that he may not be equipped to analyze correctly what is happening on the historical stage of Jewish history, or even in his own life. Our task is to accept the Torah and *mitzvot* and to do what is incumbent upon us, leaving the rest in the hands of *Hashem*. Indeed, those who draw direct connections between *aveira* A and disaster B are clearly not acting consistently with Ramban's explanation of *temimut*. Nevertheless, to the extent that *Chazal* themselves provide us with *simanim*, telling us that when we see A, B, and C, we can assume that we are in a certain period of history, there is nothing wrong with analyzing those *simanim*.

"*Avodat kelalim,*" a wider, general perspective, was given over to the *Nevi'im*, while the "*avodat peratim,*" the detail oriented, nitty gritty perspective, was given into the hands of the *Chachamim.* The *Shulchan Aruch*, which analyzes every act through the prism of Halacha and details the proper behavior in every possible situation and permutation, is *avodat peratim.* In *Hilchot Shabbat*, for example, the big picture is insufficient. The *Chachamim* are charged with teaching the technicalities of halachic life, the specific details necessary in order to properly fulfill the Torah.

The *Nevi'im*, on the other hand, had a more global view – a view of war and peace, kingship and nation, *eretz* and world. Their role was not to teach *halacha le-ma'aseh*, but rather to see where *Am Yisrael* fits on the map of history and within the spectrum of God's will. The *Nevi'im* always talk about the bigger picture; in fact, the *aveira* that they single out above all others is *avodah zarah*, which affected the entire society.

The *gemara* tells us (*Baba Batra* 12a) that "*chacham adif mi-navi,*" the wise man is of more value than the prophet. While the *navi* may have a connection to *Hashem*, he receives his inspiration directly. The *chacham*, in contrast, achieves his Torah through his own efforts and his own learning, from his own achievement. A *chacham* is preferable to a *navi* not only in the sense that he is worthy of more respect, however. Rav Kook writes that the *Chachamim* actually succeeded where the *Nevi'im* failed. "*Mah she-lo asta ha-nevuah bi-kli milchamto*" – what the *Nevi'im* failed to do with their weapons, their lectures and pleas and harangues about idolatry, murder, and immorality – the *Chachamim* were able to do through the power of their Torah. The prophets failed to uproot these terrible traits and deeds from *Klal Yisrael*, but the *Chachamim* succeeded by teaching students and transmitting the study of the law in its details. By developing the Halacha, by spreading learning, and by expanding the base of *talmidim* and bringing Torah to more and more people, the *Chachamim* were able to eliminate ignorance and stubbornness to a greater extent.

The *Nevi'im* could only stand on the mountaintops and shout; the *Chachamim*, with their small feats – raising student after student, giving *shiur* after *shiur*, writing *sefer* after *sefer* – accomplished much more. *Chacham adif mi-Navi* – the *Chachamim* were more effective in spreading Torah, and therefore in bringing the people back to *Hashem*.

At a certain point, the power of *nevuah* was removed from *Klal Yisrael* entirely. At that point, the *Chachamim* expanded their activities to the point that *nevuah* was no longer viewed as necessary. Now, the pendulum began to swing in the opposite direction. While the *Chachamim* continued to focus on the details of every aspect of Halacha, there was no longer anyone to focus on the *avodat kelalim*, no one to see the bigger picture. There was no longer anyone who was able to see *Klal Yisrael*'s place in the world. In Rav Kook's words, "*ha-kelalim heichelu le-hitrofef*" – the "big picture" issues began to weaken. They were absorbed into the *peratim* and were no longer heard from.

This will change, Rav Kook writes, in the *Acharit Ha-Yamim*, when there will be a resurgence of the *or nevuah*. At that point, the pendulum will swing once again, and "*sinat ha-peratim titgaber*" – people will come to despise the details espoused by the *Chachamim*, focusing only on the global issues. At the time of the *geulah*, when there will be a greater yearning for the power of *nevuah* and the global view of the prophets, the details offered by the *Chachamim* will be deemed insufficient and inconsequential. At that point, as our *mishnah* puts it, "*chochmat sofrim tisrach*" – the wisdom of the scholars will be deplored.

Rav Kook continues to explain other descriptions in our *mishnah* as belonging to this general pattern. "*Anshei ha-gevul yisovevu mei-ir la-ir ve-lo yechonanu*," he explains, refers to the *Chachamim*, who are the "boundary makers," those who create and maintain limits. The men of Halacha, who tell us what not to do, will be despised wherever they go. The hatred of the *Chachamim* in the *ikvata de-Mashicha* is a function of this passionate desire to see the greater picture and not to be given answers by the *Chachamim*, who provide no outlet for such passion.

As a result of this backlash against the details of the *Chachamim*, there will be a resurgence in the *or ha-nevuah*. At that time, the *Navi* will reappear and place the role of the *Chacham* in the proper perspective. Then, we will no longer be able to say that "*chacham adif mi-Navi*." When this occurs, Rav Kook concludes, "*nishmato shel Moshe tashuv le-hofia ba-olam*" – the soul of Moshe Rabbenu will reappear in the world. Moshe was both the ultimate *navi* and the ultimate *Chacham*, the Torah-giver. He combined within himself both qualities, and that synthesis will once again appear at the time of the *geulah*.

It is important to keep in mind that at the time that Rav Kook penned these lines, the revolt against Halacha and normative Judaism had already begun, and he was trying to explain how it happened. Rav Kook explains that a major contributing factor of this phenomenon was that the new generation viewed the Torah as being too restrictive. Their passion was to see a greater picture, and they shared this passion with the entire world at the turn of the 20th century. They saw a new era in which anything was possible, in which science was going to conquer the world and Jews needed to determine their own place in it. Zionism had already appeared on the world theater, and the Torah world was not responding to the new phenomena. This was the generation that Rav Kook was addressing.

Our generation is different, of course, but we can apply Rav Kook's thoughts to our own times as well.

Among many of our young people, we are beginning to sense what Rav Kook terms *"nitzotzot"* of this kind of rebellion. This type of *mered* values Judaism, but is tired of the focus on the details, on what we can and cannot do. They prefer to see the greater picture, to view *Am Yisrael, Eretz Yisrael,* and *Ha-Kadosh Baruch Hu* on a world platform. What is it all about? Where is the great vision of *deveikut* to *Ha-Kadosh Baruch Hu?*

We are witnessing an eruption within the ranks of our youth that is beginning to sound very much like what Rav Kook describes, a passionate desire to leap beyond the details and to reach a more general connection to spirituality unencumbered by specifics. This is this passion for *kelalim* that the *Chachamim* do not sufficiently address.

As a result, we face a grave danger – that our fixation on *peratim,* while these youngsters desire the *kelalim,* will ultimately lead them to stray outside the norm. That's something that we, as parents and as leaders, must certainly worry about.

∾ RESPONDING TO THE PROBLEM

How should we respond to this problem? Rav Kook suggests that once the surge has taken place, it is better to leave it alone. It is useless to yell and scream about how those rebelling are acting inappropriately. This will not control the *hitpartzut*, but rather only make it stronger.

We can extrapolate from Rav Kook's discussion to the situation in our own generation. There are things that are going on within our youth that are perhaps not what we would expect or want. How should we deal with it? Should we ostracize and ex-communicate? Should we throw them out or should we understand? This tension is part and parcel of the way we must look at our society today. Neither response is necessarily entirely wrong or right.[37]

On the one hand, we should admire the strength, vitality, and passion that we find in some of our youth today, their passion and desire to explore new ways of reconnecting with *Yahadut* in a way that will be meaningful to them. On the other hand, this trend is troublesome in the sense that it has to be controlled; it must be prevented from getting lost in activities that are not normative at all. And along with this

---

37 I was recently at a wedding and I commented to a Rav there how I admired the intensity of the young peoples' dancing. The Rav acknowledged that it was indeed impressive – but he said that he was nevertheless very concerned about the phenomenon. This is exactly the tension we are discussing.

passion has come an upsurge in the rejection of authority which cannot be condoned.

But what are we to do about it? Do we simply say, *"Ein lanu al mi le-hisha'ein elah al Avinu she-ba-shamayim?"* Do we say, "It's the *ikvata de-Mashicha* and *chutzpa* is supposed to explode?" Should we sit back and wait for things to work themselves out, or should we take this bull by the horns and direct it in a way that will make these new phenomena constructive?

No matter how we choose to deal with these developments, we must remember that the processes that we are seeing in some of our youth today are inevitable consequences of the historical development of Torah and Halacha. Sensitive souls will sometimes not find their avenue within the *avodat ha-peratim*, the nitty gritty of Halacha, and will need to find another route to express their passionate Yiddishkeit, the *avodat ha-kelalim*. Since there are no *Nevi'im* to direct this passionate worldview, the effect may not be constructive unless we do something about it.

❧ LESSONS FOR US

I believe that we can also learn a lesson for ourselves from this phenomenon. We might be tempted to think of this as someone else's problem – perhaps that of others' children, and perhaps that of the professionals who deal with them – but not our own. We are tempted to declare, "This is deviant and we have to somehow deal with this deviance." This is true in a certain sense, but nevertheless, we can also learn something from it at the same time.

Complacency, feeling safe in one's comfort zone, is the enemy of *teshuvah* because it entails that there is no reason to change. Furthermore, it leads one to a sense of having the right to judge others who have not reached my place or level. I assume that only my perspective is correct and legitimate, and that is therefore clearly the perspective that everyone else should have as well. Complacent people are truly committed to Torah and *mitzvoth*, but they see no reason to change. This is who I am. This is what I am. This is where I am, and this is where I will be.

Rav Kook talks about this at length in his *Orot Ha-Teshuvah*. *Teshuva* is not only the process of correcting ones' sins; it is also a constant process of movement from one level to the next, from a lower level to a higher one. When one stops moving, when one declares that he has arrived, he is not fulfilling the *mitzvah* of *teshuvah*, which applies to all people – not only sinners. Even if one has somehow repented for every sin on his list, that is not the end of *Hilchot Teshuva*. *Teshuva* means being unsatisfied, being restless, unwilling to accept one's current situation as being the ultimate that he can achieve.

There may be many things wrong with the direction of some of our youth, but there is one thing that is clearly right – their passion to reconnect on a spiritual level to the deepest roots of *Yahadut*. We should learn from them not to allow ourselves to wallow in complacency.

We note our desire to break out of our set ways and to reawaken our passion for Torah every time we say *Shemoneh Esrei*. In *Elokai Netzor*, we ask *Hashem*, "*Petach libi be-Toratecha*," open my heart to Your Torah. We do not ask that He open our minds, but our hearts. Torah should be something that our hearts should desire, not simply an intellectual exercise. "*Ve-acharei mitzvotecha tirdof nafshi*" – we should run after *mitzvot,* not simply do them. We implore *Hashem* to give us back the passion for Torah and *mitzvot.*

Interestingly, Rambam dedicates most of his *Hilchot Teshuva* to discussing the *avodat peratim,* the details of *teshuva* – *viduy, charata, kabbala le-atid,* the different types of forgiveness, etc. At the end of *Hilchot Teshuva,* however, he switches to a discussion of *avodat kelalim,* discussing repentance in much broader strokes. It is in *Hilchot Teshuva* – not *Hilchot Dei'ot* or *Hilchot Yesodei Ha-Torah* – that he discusses serving *Hashem* out of love. It is there that he describes what true *ahavat Hashem* entails, describing it as even more powerful than human love:

"It entails that he should love *Hashem* a great and overpowering love, to the point that his soul is connected to love of *Hashem* and he finds himself enthralled by it at all times, like one who is lovesick and whose thoughts do not depart from that particular woman, whether he is sitting or standing or eating or drinking... Greater than this is the love for *Hashem.*"

In order to properly complete the process of *teshuva,* one must serve *Hashem* out of love.

Passion is not something that one can simply turn on or off with a switch. It's something that has to grow within you, something that has to develop. It is not simply about doing more than one was doing before, although that is obviously an important part of *teshuva.* Everyone has realms in Torah and *mitzvot* in which they can improve. But going to *minyan* or a *shiur* more often – which are certainly important steps – will not necessarily increase the passion that we are talking about. The *teshuva* I am referring to entails a shift of consciousness. We must accept the fact that we can never be comfortable with our *avodas Hashem*, never satisfied with what we've accomplished at any given moment in time. This *teshuva* entails a switch in the way that we think about Yiddishkeit, making it central to our lives to the point that everything else is secondary. This is a much greater change than adding this or that additional *mitzvah* commitment.

This is what Rambam is talking about at the end of *Hilchot Teshuvah*, and this is one of the messages that we should be hearing from our youth. They are teaching us to bring back the passion to our *Yahadut*, looking at everything through the glasses of *Yahadut* and spiritual awakening. Once we hear that message, we can at least accept the fact that the passion is missing.

One simple way to start along the path is to simply focus on what we're saying when we *daven*. If we make an effort to understand the words and not mindlessly recite them, if we think about what we mean instead of thinking about work or why the *chazzan* is going so slowly, if we concentrate on the drama of the *"ofanim ve-chayot ha-kodesh"* who stand in Heaven and praise *Hashem* – that would be a wonderful beginning to the shift we need to see in our *Yahadut*.

The Vilna Gaon and the Chafetz Chaim – neither of whom could be accused of being Chassidim – wrote that the *geulah* will only come when *Klal Yisrael* begins to look into the *sodot* of Torah. This searching must be directed and controlled, but it cannot be ignored. If we ignore the processes of *geulah* that are taking place in our generation, then we may be defeating that very process. If we absorb the message from our youth, if we learn to share their passion, we may thereby regain their respect and win them back. If we speak their language – the language of passion for Judaism – we can turn our youth around.

www.ingramcontent.com/pod-product-compliance
Lightning Source LLC
LaVergne TN
LVHW051128080426
835510LV00018B/2290